Teaching the Classics in the Inclusive Classroom

Reader Response Activities to Engage All Learners

**Katherine S. McKnight
and Bradley P. Berlage**

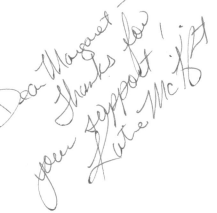

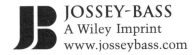

JOSSEY-BASS
A Wiley Imprint
www.josseybass.com

Copyright © 2008 by John Wiley & Sons, Inc. All rights reserved.

Published by Jossey-Bass.
A Wiley Imprint
989 Market Street, San Francisco, CA 94103-1741—www.josseybass.com

No part of this publication may be reproduced, stored in a retrieval system, or transmitted in any form or by any means, electronic, mechanical, photocopying, recording, scanning, or otherwise, except as permitted under Section 107 or 108 of the 1976 United States Copyright Act, without either the prior written permission of the publisher, or authorization through payment of the appropriate per-copy fee to the Copyright Clearance Center, Inc., 222 Rosewood Drive, Danvers, MA 01923, 978-750-8400, fax 978-646-8600, or on the Web at www.copyright.com. Requests to the publisher for permission should be addressed to the Permissions Department, John Wiley & Sons, Inc., 111 River Street, Hoboken, NJ 07030, 201-748-6011, fax 201-748-6008, or online at www.wiley.com/go/permissions.

Readers should be aware that Internet Web sites offered as citations and/or sources for further information may have changed or disappeared between the time this was written and when it is read.

Limit of Liability/Disclaimer of Warranty: While the publisher and author have used their best efforts in preparing this book, they make no representations or warranties with respect to the accuracy or completeness of the contents of this book and specifically disclaim any implied warranties of merchantability or fitness for a particular purpose. No warranty may be created or extended by sales representatives or written sales materials. The advice and strategies contained herein may not be suitable for your situation. You should consult with a professional where appropriate. Neither the publisher nor author shall be liable for any loss of profit or any other commercial damages, including but not limited to special, incidental, consequential, or other damages.

Jossey-Bass books and products are available through most bookstores. To contact Jossey-Bass directly call our Customer Care Department within the U.S. at 800-956-7739, outside the U.S. at 317-572-3986, or fax 317-572-4002.

Jossey-Bass also publishes its books in a variety of electronic formats. Some content that appears in print may not be available in electronic books.

Library of Congress Cataloging-in-Publication Data

McKnight, Katherine S. (Katherine Siewert)
    Teaching the classics in the inclusive classroom : reader response activities to engage all learners / Katherine S. McKnight, Bradley P. Berlage.
        p. cm.
    Includes bibliographical references and index.
    ISBN 978-0-7879-9406-8 (alk. paper)
    1. Reading (Secondary)—United States. 2. Literature—Study and teaching (Secondary)—United States. 3. Inclusive education—United States. I. Berlage, Bradley P., 1962- II. Title.
        LB1632.M36 2007
        428.4071′2—dc22

                                                                2007019901

Printed in the United States of America
FIRST EDITION
PB Printing   10 9 8 7 6 5 4 3 2 1

Contents

Part One: Teaching the Classics to All Students

Part Two: Working with Selected Classic Texts

For all English teachers

For Jim, Ellie and Colin—they are the loves of my life
—Katherine S. McKnight

For my family—extended and nuclear
—Bradley Berlage

For our students—past, present and future

Acknowledgements

Katie began her teaching career in Fairfax County, Virginia. She would not meet Brad Berlage, working next door, for nearly two decades. It was serendipitous that they met in Chicago and then joined forces to co-author this volume.

We need to acknowledge from the onset, Louise Rosenblatt, who is the muse for this book and much of our teaching. Through her writing, she advocated for democracy in our English classrooms and we carry her spirit in our teaching.

We would also like to thank our editor, Margie McAnneny, for her enthusiasm and support of this project and Justin Frahm, for his expertise during the production phase of this book and his infectious humor. This book would not have been realized without the assistance of our teacher colleagues and the many students that we have taught in the Chicago area.

Introduction: "This Old Stuff Ain't So Bad"

Katie shares these experiences from her own high school memories:

> When I was a student in high school, I had very few opportunities to freely respond to literature in my English classes. My teachers deemed responses acceptable only if I agreed with the literary critics or the teacher's manual. As the student, I waited for this information to "trickle down" to me. Even if I referred to the text for support, I was often told that it was a "good attempt" but I was "off track." For the most part, I was a student of "top-down" literature study — the teacher's interpretation was at the "top" and his or her comments and analysis was the prevailing authority.

Brad shares a story of his experience with the literary canon in high school:

> In my high school English classes, I remember having to read a lot of the classics, such as *Look Homeward, Angel; The Great Gatsby;* and *The Old Man and the Sea.* When we discussed them or were tested on them, there was only one correct answer, and that was the interpretation the teacher provided. I never could come up with the answer the teacher was looking for and ended up doodling my way through the literary canon. In high school, I never enjoyed studying the classics or felt confident in my ability in this area. I am sure that is why, at the time, I hated reading classical literature and was much more engaged in studying math and computers. It was not until I got to college, and the teacher invited us to provide our *own* interpretation of what we read, that I actually started enjoying studying literature. What a wild turn my life took after that. After a few years in college, I ended up switching my major from math to English and later pursued my master's degree in order to teach English.

The "Green" Teacher

As a student teacher entering the profession, Katie attended a conference for teachers of English. As a pre-service teacher, she listened intently as one of the conference presenters shared his wisdom: "Students do not read the traditional canonical works that teachers assign," he stated. "Canonical works do not relate to their experiences as modern teenagers because the language is too hard for them."

It seemed that many people in the audience agreed with the presenter on this point, and because Katie was just entering the profession, with no practical experience

Self-Reflection
Reflect back on your experience in the high school English classroom. What was it like when you studied the classics? Did you enjoy studying *Beowulf* in high school? Were you able to understand the complexities of *The Great Gatsby* or Homer's *The Odyssey?* How did your teacher present the information to you?

to weigh this against, she figured this must just be the way it is. So during her first few years of teaching, Katie taught the literary canon using the methods traditionally used—vocabulary lists, multiple-choice questions, matching quizzes, and terminology sheets. Her students seemed bored, but based on the advice she'd received early on, she really didn't expect them to be enjoying these classic works. "The literary canon is too hard for them," Katie thought.

As an English teacher for over a decade in a diverse and public city high school, Katie desperately sought ways in which she could make authors like Chaucer, Shakespeare, Frederick Douglass, Cervantes, and Jane Austen come alive for her students. As she became more comfortable in her role as a teacher, Katie started to branch out and use a variety of strategies when teaching the canon.

After implementing the kinds of teaching strategies that are described in this book, her sophomore students, who were previously bored with the text, now relished the suspense and terror of Edgar Allan Poe. Katie's students begged for more, as they unlocked the vocabulary and linguistic complexity of the canon through active, integrated, language-arts-learning activities.

Katie decided to apply these same strategies with her high school juniors, who were reading *Macbeth* and struggling with the Elizabethan language of Shakespeare's theater. Using reader's theater, as one of the strategies outlined in this book, her juniors performed key scenes from the play; then, they too begged to read more canonical works.

"What's wrong with these kids?" Katie thought. Her students eagerly digested *Othello* and convinced her to take them on a field trip to see Shakespeare on stage. Fumi, the student ringleader in the class, declared, "This old stuff ain't so bad."

Katie discovered that not only were her students reading the canonical works but also they were understanding, appreciating, and even *enjoying* the literature they were reading and wanted more. Thinking it was a fluke, Katie

tried these strategies again with another group of students the following quarter, and the same result occurred: interested, engaged students.

She realized that the problem *wasn't* that students couldn't comprehend the text. They could, in fact, become engaged with the classic texts. The problem—Katie saw clearly then—was the teaching method being used. Once she decided to pitch the study-guide questions and vocabulary lists and replace them with teaching strategies that incorporated the reader-response theory (the theory behind the strategies described in this book), students became charged up about "this old stuff." The literary canon was *not* too difficult for her students to read, understand, and appreciate, when they felt connected to the text.

The History of Teaching the Classics

The scope of the literary canon—the classics taught in the schools—has not changed much over the years. Most of the same books that were taught seventy-five years ago when high schools first became open to the general public are still being taught in high schools today. Children did not actually start studying literature in high schools until the 1920s. In fact, American public high schools did not become fully inclusive to all students—boys, girls, and diverse populations—until after World War II.

In many ways, the teaching of the literary canon in the American public high school system is still in its infancy. As a result, the *way* the classics are taught has largely remained the same. Due to the relatively short time period in the American history of the inclusive public classroom, the pedagogical tradition of teaching the literary canon as "artifact," using the "top-down" theory mentioned earlier, has been maintained. It is time to change this pedagogical tradition and replace it with one that is more effective for the inclusive classroom of the twenty-first century.

Problems with the Traditional Method of Teaching the Classics

The method we use to *teach* the classics directs our students as to the method they will use to *read* the classics. In turn, this affects how they perceive and understand the literary canon. Almost *all* of us start out teaching the canon using these traditional tools.

As we (Katie and Brad) were preparing material for this book, we spent one summer day going through our file folders of relevant archival material used to supplement our teaching strategies. This is how it sometimes went:

Every once in a while, Katie would groan as she found some tests or study guides from her early years. "God, this is awful!" she yelled, throwing the files in the trash. Brad would then pull the files from the trash and put them into piles. Katie found another multiple-choice test and tossed it into the circular file that Brad proceeded to pull back out. "Stop it!" Katie laughed, but she was serious as well. Finally, after

Brad's unrelenting perseverance, she realized Brad was right. As important as it is to show the end product of this pedagogical change, it is just as important to share the growing process experienced along the way.

In order to provide examples of the traditional methods of teaching the classics, as well as provide the benefits and drawbacks of these tools, we've included the results of some of Brad's dumpster-diving efforts, which exemplify our own traditional method for teaching the classics.

Examples of Traditional Teaching

Multiple-Choice Question — *The Great Gatsby:* "The <u>supercilious</u> assumption was that on Sunday afternoon I had nothing better to do."
(A) agreeable   (B) silly   (C) disdainful

Multiple-Choice Question — *Hamlet:* The ghost warns Hamlet not to
(A) hurt Ophelia   (B) forget him   (C) take revenge on him

"Right There" Question — *Macbeth:* "In the opening scene of *Macbeth*, the three witches show Macbeth three apparitions/ghosts. What pronouncements do they make?"

Vocabulary lists, literary terms, multiple-choice tests, and study guides are tools for literature *study*, but they do not provide the keys for a student to unlock a personal connection with canonical literature (see Exhibit I.1).

So often, as English teachers, we use the classroom to analyze a "great work" to such a depth that we forget the connections and stories that drew us to the classic text in the first place. Although this traditional teaching method allows students to search for responses to specific questions, this style of reading limits a student's ability to engage and connect with the text. The teacher using these traditional methods of teaching the classics asks the kinds of analysis questions that will become part of an exam a few weeks from the lesson.

Self-Reflection
Reflect back again to your own personal experience in a high school English class. When you studied Shakespeare, were you asked what you *thought* of a passage or what Shakespeare was *saying* in the passage? Was there only one right answer to your teacher's questions?

Exhibit I.1 Traditional Teaching Methods for the Classics

Efferent Teaching Tools	Benefits	Drawbacks
Vocabulary lists Literary terms lists Study guides Multiple-choice tests Matching tests	Can be repeated or copied in a quick, timely manner Address lower-order cognitive skills Address needs for basic study skills	May not place vocabulary in context Do not address multiple learning styles Do not provide real-world scenarios Only one right answer Severely limit aesthetic reading and engagement in text Do not promote higher-ordered thinking

A friend and teaching colleague years ago referred to this style of teaching literature as "frog-dissected literature study." When we teach literature in this manner and ask students solely about the structure of the work, we often "dissect" a literary work for our students to the point where it is unrecognizable.

Reflecting on our early use of traditional teaching methods to teach the canon, we are quick to share that after using these new strategies, not only did our students enjoy learning the classics but also we enjoyed teaching the classics using the strategies outlined in this book. Of course, our students became aware of our increased enthusiasm and, in turn, became more engaged in the literature.

Wilhelm (1997) references the "pedagogical tradition" of "teach[ing] literature by asking students a set of questions about the form and content of a work" (p. 122). Although teachers mean well, many require students to read in this manner and look for one answer. Louise Rosenblatt (1904–2005), the foundational theorist for reader response, defines this method of reading as *efferent reading*, which is characterized by reading that focuses on "selecting out and analytically abstracting the information or ideas or directions of actions that will remain when the reading is over" (p. 32). If students read efferently, they rarely go beyond the structure of the text and are unlikely to experience a text aesthetically.

Asking students solely about the structure of a work does not offer them the chance to experience the text aesthetically. As Rosenblatt (1993) argues, the potentially aesthetic literary experience can be destroyed if we constantly pick a literary work apart, thereby denying our students any chance of personally connecting with the text.

To help students succeed academically with classical literature and develop an interest in classical literature, we need to help them believe they can read and comprehend the classics, as well as enhance their own engagement with the material.

Promoting Student Engagement and Self-Efficacy

Rosenblatt (1995) argues, "Literature must have some connection to students' lives" (p. 34). Once this connection is established "between the work and their own lives, it is easier to get them to think about other ideas or connections in the novel" (p. xv).

Many factors need to be present for students to be academically engaged. But if they *are* academically engaged, they are not simply committed to completing their class assignments or to achieving grades; they are emotionally invested in the learning process (Newmann, 1992). In addition, one of the most critical components is students' self-efficacy, that is, their own belief in their ability to succeed academically. The chart in Figure I.1 exemplifies the framework for learning the classics in the inclusive classroom and is based on models developed by Newmann (1992) and Linnenbrink and Pintrich (2003).

When teaching the classics, students' belief in their own ability to comprehend the material plays a key role in their ability to become engaged with the material. If the learning environment nurtures students' belief in their own academic ability, that environment also facilitates their behavioral, cognitive, and motivational engagement in the classroom (Linnenbrink and Pintrich, 2003; Pintrich and De Groot, 1990). This directly affects students' ability to learn and achieve (Smith, 2004).

As illustrated graphically in Figure I.1, students' success or failure in the area of learning and achievement has a circular effect, ultimately re-affecting their own feeling of self-efficacy. Teaching strategies, such as the ones outlined in this book, can motivate students reading the classics because they promote student self-efficacy, as has been reported by many teachers over the years.

The Aesthetic Style of Teaching the Classics

As literature teachers, we must bear in mind that not only is reading literature an aesthetic and literary experience, it is also a personal experience. To elicit this engagement in our students, we must allow them to develop a personal connection with the text.

Rosenblatt (1993) defines the experience of reading literature that captures our human impulses as *aesthetic reading*. In aesthetic reading, the reader's attention is centered directly on what he or she is living through during a relationship with a particular text (Rosenblatt, 1978). These aesthetic

Self-Reflection
Think back to when you first started to enjoy reading classical literature. If you read it in school, did the teacher allow you to develop your own personal connection with the literature? Were you allowed to share your personal thoughts or feelings about the literature in class? Did your teacher validate your shared thoughts and feelings?

Teaching the Classics in the Inclusive Classroom

Figure I.1 Impact of Teaching Style on Student Self-Efficacy and Academic Achievement

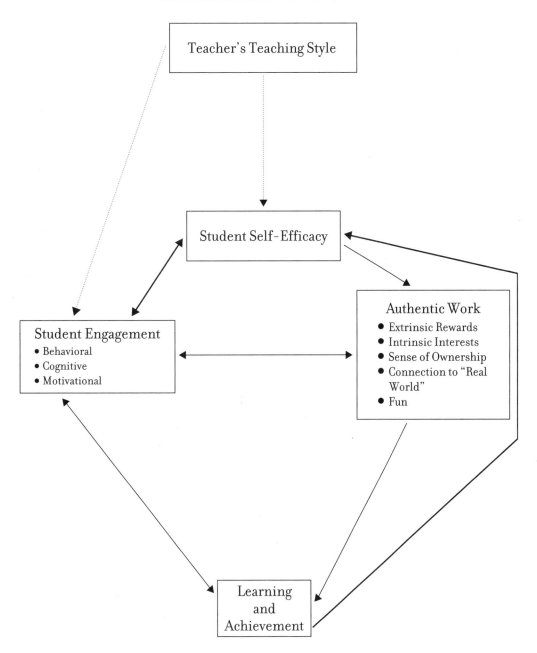

experiences of reading a text lead to personal and emotional responses for the reader and are the seeds for the creation of lifelong readers.

Reader-Response Theory

The teaching strategies that we have found to be effective in teaching the canon are based in reader-response theory—the brainchild of Louise Rosenblatt, who

Figure I.2   Rosenblatt's Transactional Theory

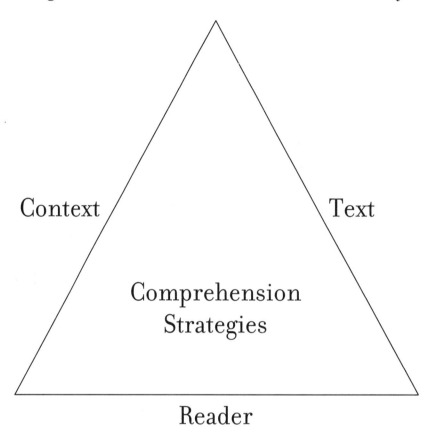

argued the merits of the classics, or the literary canon. Reader-response theory (see Figure I.2) allows and encourages students to provide their own interpretation of literature in order for them to build and add to their current experiences. In contrast with traditional teaching methodology, reader-response-based instruction promotes a dynamic relationship between the reader and the text.

A reader who is actively involved in the text develops an understanding that is exhibited in individual responses. Rosenblatt argues that through literature instruction, teachers must create better readers rather than convince their students of one correct interpretation. Reader-response instruction asserts that there are differences among readers and texts, and allows for the possibility of more than one response to a text.

Today, the reader-response method is being used in study guides for teaching most young-adult literature, such as *Bud, Not Buddy; The Outsiders;* or *Loser;* because young-adult literature focuses on more current themes and settings, students can relate to more easily than the themes and settings in the classics. In addition, the language and vocabulary in young-adult literature is in a format that students are more comfortable with. Although these factors do increase student engagement with the text, the teaching method used with

young-adult literature—reader response—facilitates students' connection to the text. Whether or not the setting and theme of *The Outsiders* is one that interests students, it is certain that they would not connect with the material aesthetically if their teachers used traditional teaching methods, such as giving them multiple-choice tests or fill-in-the-blank quizzes.

As Peck (1989) explains, "Adolescent readers respond best to literature when discussion of it starts within the circle of their own experience, and they can begin their reading by relating it to the work personally and emotionally" (p. xv). The challenge of canonical literature is not an obstacle for students; rather, the method we use to teach them is the roadblock preventing them from connecting with the text. Canonical authors can offer an aesthetic experience for students if they are given the opportunity to respond personally and emotionally to these texts (Bloom, 1995; Rosenblatt, 1993).

Pre-Reading, During-Reading, and Post-Reading Strategies

By incorporating the kinds of pre-reading, during-reading, and post-reading strategies that are based on reader-response theory and that make up the heart of this book, we allow our students to relate to the classics, even though the students themselves are modern teenagers. Urban high school students we have taught, regardless of ability level or special need, were perfectly capable of experiencing the passion of canonical literature on their own level. As their understanding deepened, all the students discovered their own personal voice in the canon and a desire to read more of the classics.

When students are encouraged to read the classics aesthetically, they can

- Actively participate in literature
- Become aware of associations, feelings, attitudes, and ideas conveyed in literature
- Synthesize these elements into a meaningful structure
- Live through, reflect on, and criticize their own responses to the text
- Understand the complexity of the world through the eyes of different authors
- Grow in partnership and wisdom of the past and aspirations for the future of our culture and our society

Reading and understanding literature is something like unpacking boxes after moving to a new home. The individual chooses how and where to place the items, thus creating a schema for the new surroundings. The "old stuff ain't so bad" if we, as teachers, create learning environments that nurture students' personal and emotional responses to text, allowing them to create their own schema for the classics. When we encourage students to explore, experiment, and "unpack" linguistically challenging text, the reading experience becomes an engaging, empowering experience for both the teacher and the student.

Putting These Strategies into Action

In any middle or high school English class, students have numerous and varied responses and reactions to a given text (see Exhibit I.2).

These responses can be influenced by a number of different conditions, such as students' previous experiences, age, gender, learning styles, special needs, cultural differences, and current circumstances.

Intrinsic goals are linked closely to individual growth tendencies. As a result, when teachers teaching the classics link learning to their students' intrinsic goals, rather than to the teacher's own extrinsic goals, the teacher promotes "a more integrative and conceptual processing of the learning material" (Vansteenkiste, Simons, Lens, Soenens, and Matos, 2005, p. 17).

As displayed in Figure I.1, classroom conditions that support a sense of ownership and competency can also facilitate intrinsic motivation.

When Katie's students made the following statements, they articulated this personal and emotional response to a text:

"Man, does Othello know that Iago is bad?"

"Hamlet is just like Bigger Thomas. They're both so isolated and alone, they resort to violence to solve their problems."

"Forget it, Romeo and Juliet aren't real. Love at first sight doesn't exist."

Exhibit I.2 Influences on Students' Responses to Text

Students' responses to text are influenced by
Previous experiences
Age
Gender
Cultural differences
Current social context
Current events
Individual learning styles
Community current events

Teaching the Classics in the Inclusive Classroom

This is the first step toward students' comprehension of the text. As students describe their opinions, empathy, or disgust, they are becoming aware, as readers, of how they are experiencing a text. Once students begin to feel this personal and emotional involvement with a text, they develop a deeper understanding of the themes, characters, and events in a literary work.

Katie told her juniors, as they read *Macbeth* and complained throughout the first act: "Sure it's hard, but Mount Everest can't be climbed in one day." In turn, they persevered and were proud of themselves when they were able to read *Othello* independently the following quarter. If the expectation that students can read difficult text is not established, students such as these will probably not develop the confidence to read another Shakespearean play. If students are given the opportunity to respond to a text personally, however, it is logical to assume that they at least have the potential to become more vested in their reading experiences.

A teacher's instructional belief system has a direct effect on students' ability to learn and achieve. Students can become engaged in challenging literature if they are allowed to respond and are no longer required to play the game, "What's the right answer?" *Any* kind of literature can be engaging if students have the opportunity to feel some connection with the text, as well as to voice their own understanding and interpretation of it.

So how can teachers of classical literature nurture *all* their students to become academically engaged in an inclusive middle or high school English class? Teachers need practical classroom strategies and methods based in sound pedagogical theory in order to promote engagement with literature.

For these transactions between students and classical literature to happen, several provisions must be in place:

- The reader must be able to decode the text's "surface structure"—the letters and words on a page (Kariolides, 1992; Smith, 2004).
- The text (or surface structure) must be understandable to the reader so that he or she can transition from the surface structure to the "deep structure"—the meaning that the reader constructs (Kariolides, 1992; Smith, 2004).
- Most important, the reader must be an active participant in exploring the text (Rosenblatt, 1993; Kariolides, 1992).

After implementing the strategies laid out in this book, teachers will see their students grow through the following stages:

Stages of Student Participation

1. Students make superfluous remarks about the classical literature, testing the waters to see if their remarks are accepted and validated.
2. Students continue to practice their feedback, increasing their level of engagement, as well as their metacognitive participation.

3. Students become aware that *their* opinion of literature matters in the classroom, further increasing their metacognitive participation, engagement, and academic achievement.

These stages occur as the students learn to trust their teacher's validation and acceptance of students' participation. It can take as long as a full quarter or semester for students to get through stage 1, but teachers will see a huge improvement in student engagement and performance once that trust is created.

The following chapters provide specific strategies to achieve these goals, based in reader-response theory, for all students in the inclusive middle or high school English classroom. Using the strategies we outline in this book, teachers can invite students to challenge their ability to think, reason, and become part of the imaginative world of text (Rosenblatt, 1993). Through the use of these tools, students can learn to "unpack" linguistically complex text.

Part One

Teaching the Classics to All Students

Student Voice, Discussion, and Lecture

> In 1930, the Republican-controlled House of Representatives, in an effort to alleviate the effects of the ... Anyone? Anyone? ... the Great Depression, passed the ... Anyone? Anyone? The tariff bill?..."
>
> Economics teacher to a silent class in *Ferris Bueller's Day Off*

Benjamin Stein's portrayal of an economics teacher answering his own questions in a disinterested class was hilarious in the movie *Ferris Bueller's Day Off;* however we, as teachers, have all experienced this at one time or another, where we can almost hear crickets chirping due to the deathly silence in our classroom. Attempting to engage our students in in-depth discussions can, at times, be like pulling teeth.

It is hard to believe that teachers need to develop techniques to encourage students to talk in the classroom, when we can witness lively conversations at almost any time in the school hallways. However, when they walk into many classrooms, students often become stifled while trying to speak in the more formalized setting, especially when academic discussion is expected.

How do we encourage student talk that contributes to a lively and engaging language arts classroom? Many factors shape student talk in a classroom other than the main curricular focus—English. More schools are linguistically diverse than ever before, and this can have an impact on classroom discourse. Students who appear to be disinterested in or resistant to school can also present challenges. As classroom teachers, we face the occasional student who *refuses* to respond or participate in classroom discussions, no matter how lively and adolescent-relevant they may seem to us.

In many classrooms, academic discussion is not the norm for a number of reasons. These reasons may include a belief that

- The students are not interested or they are not mature enough to participate.
- The language barriers of the students prevent them from interacting in a class discussion.
- Special needs students will not be able to participate because of their educational deficiencies.
- These students do not have the ability to think more deeply.
- The current pedagogical or administrative paradigm does not support class discussion and focuses more on test achievement.
- There is not enough time in the period to hold a discussion.

As a result, we may find ourselves posing questions to our students, then answering the questions ourselves in order to speed up the "learning process." This results in turning our goal of having classroom discussions into giving teacher-directed lectures. Although teacher-directed lectures provide us with a large amount of control over the material covered and the speed in which to do so, lecturing provides the teacher with only *limited* ability to motivate, engage, and connect with the material by building on students' current schema. As we know, for developing a higher level of understanding and long-term comprehension, it is essential that students become active participants in the learning process, in order to build on their current schema, instead of memorizing facts, words, and dates, and other information that is imparted by a teacher. To do this, we must create learner-centered discussion.

Teacher-directed lectures, so characteristic of the traditional classroom, are not conducive to the current model for teaching the English language arts. With chalk in hand, the teacher talks and the students dutifully take notes. Please note, however, that there are times when lecture is effective, but lecturing is only one teaching strategy, and others are needed. If this is the only method that a teacher uses in the classroom, a student who may have learned through other teaching or instructional techniques may not have had the opportunity to learn the content. When students are not encouraged or allowed to speak in class, it can create barriers in a classroom. An integrated language arts teaching model encourages hands-on experiences and opportunities for the teacher and students to share knowledge, as skills in the language arts are honed. In addition, an effective classroom discussion is the cornerstone for the effectiveness of the other strategies outlined in this book.

In this section, we address

Questioning: how to create effective questions for the classroom

Promoting class discussion: how to create an environment that promotes productive and engaging class discussions for any situation and group of students

Questioning

Asking, answering, and discussing questions allows us to explore and represent our thoughts and ideas. How do we create and ask questions that encourage students to explore their ideas in newly presented content? Effective questions engage students in dialogue and exploration (see Exhibit 1.1).

Now that we have identified the characteristics of effective questions, let's look at the possible *types* of questions.

Exhibit 1.1   Characteristics of Effective Questions

Effective Questions

Allow students to react and explore ideas.

Prompt students to examine different points of view and a variety of topics.

Offer experiences for students that allow them to take the lead in classroom discussions.

Create a classroom learning environment where students interact with each other.

Provide the teacher with information about the students' learning and comprehension.

Create learning communities where students are willing to contribute, question, explore, challenge and take intellectual risks.

Provide the opportunity for ALL students to become engaged, irregardless of their ability level

Real and Pseudo Questions

Questions carry the potential for students to explore and understand material. We often write questions in the margins of our schoolbooks, as we seek understanding of the new content. Real questions that prompt student inquiry and exploration are not as easy to develop as they may seem. Many novice teachers tend to write pseudo questions (ones for which the teacher already has a specific answer in mind) or "closed questions," which require only a yes-or-no answer or an answer directly from the text. These kinds of questions must be avoided because they do not promote higher-order thinking for students or engage students in their own learning.

Not only do we need to understand the difference between real and pseudo questions, we must consider creating *questioning hierarchies*, that is, progressions of questions that lead students through different levels of thinking.

Questioning Hierarchies

Most questioning hierarchies begin with simple recall, or lower-level thinking questions. From this point, the hierarchies (presumably) transition to questions and prompts that require critical and higher-level thinking skills. However, anyone who has taught knows that this is simply not true. Students interact with new material from a variety of angles and approaches, especially in an English classroom.

Leila Christenbury tackles the notion of questioning hierarchies in her book *Questioning: A Path to Critical Thinking* (1983), coauthored with Patricia Kelly, and more recently in *Making the Journey: Being and Becoming a Teacher of English Language Arts* (1994). She argues that the questioning circle is a more useful model for constructing questions.

The questioning circle model adopts the notion that one's schema are not sequential or hierarchical. The model is made up of three areas: the subject matter, personal reality, and external reality. Christenbury (1994) explains that "These areas overlap—as does knowledge—and are not ordered" (p. 207).

The areas overlap, as Christenbury argues, because knowledge itself is not ordered and isolated. For novice teachers, the model is useful because the goal of any classroom discussion is for the students to explore higher-level questions, as represented by the overlapping shaded areas in the model. These higher-level and more meaningful questions can be reached through any of the three paths represented by the individual circles: the matter, personal reality, and external reality. Teachers should create and generate questions that are from each of these areas, in addition to the overlapping areas.

In order for students to be engaged in any meaningful classroom discussion, they need to have personal and meaningful questions posed to them. Pseudo (what's-on-the-teacher's-mind) questions and closed (yes-no) questions cannot accomplish this level of student engagement or critical thinking. As teachers, we must encourage our students to ask and respond to challenging questions. This does not always occur, especially in urban schools where larger class sizes and other issues come into play. The level of challenge for questions in urban classrooms has been most recently studied in the Chicago public schools.

Many books and teacher development materials have been created to hone teachers' questioning skills. Here are five suggestions for developing effective questions:

1. Avoid closed, or yes-no questions.
2. Do not use what's-on-the-teacher's-mind questions, as they do not engage students in class discussions.
3. Be as clear as possible when posing questions for the students. Asking more than one question in the same sentence can confuse students; it may be unclear what you are asking.
4. Avoid creating questions that reveal the answers: the teacher states the obvious, asks a question, and the student confirms the information.

5. Avoid unclear and vague questions that will undoubtedly hinder a classroom discussion.

Teacher-Directed Questions

Although we advocate that students be encouraged to ask questions and promote inquiry in the classroom, this does not mean that the teacher dwells in the shadows and does not ask questions. The teacher facilitates and promotes discussion and inquiry with the students. We caution that a learning community that reflects the tenets of an integrated English language arts classroom is not dominated by teacher-directed questions; these are components but are not a sole focus.

Here are three strategies that promote student inquiry and build the learning community:

First, ask open-ended questions; they encourage the students to explore a wide variety of ideas and possibilities. Because the open-ended question leaves the composition of the answer to the respondent, it promotes thoughtful reflection and higher-level thinking.

Second, ask a variety of questions that include divergent and convergent inquiries. Convergent questions are generally simpler and often require the respondent to confirm some fact or information. The divergent question promotes higher-level thinking skills and often requires the student to develop a more creative or uniquely insightful answer. Think of convergent questions as a way of warming up students before they even consider divergent questions.

And third, be patient if a student does not respond right away. Give the student an opportunity to respond and consider the question that you posed. Model patience for your students.

Remember: teacher-directed questions promote student inquiry and contribute to, rather than detract from, an engaging learning community.

Student-Directed Questions

Just as teacher-directed questions are a vital part of building an engaging learning community, student-directed questions are a key component as well. If encouraging students to ask questions is desirable behavior in an English language arts classroom, then it is critical for the teacher to create an atmosphere in which students are not afraid to ask questions for fear of embarrassment or peer ridicule.

Creating an Environment for Effective Class Discussion

Student-centered discussion does not mean that "anything goes." It means that, unlike teacher-centered discussions, the focus of the discussion is not controlled by the teacher; in student-centered discussions, the students are invited to orchestrate the classroom discourse. Index card questions, discussion

groups, and student-led discussions are a few strategies for helping this to occur. More strategies will be addressed throughout the text.

Both oral and written language are powerful tools for learning. In examining oral language as a strategy for instruction, we must recognize its power to enable us to explain, represent, and interpret our own experiences. As Bruner (1975) suggests, language is a tool for thought, and we need to employ teaching strategies for this phenomenon to occur in our students.

Large-group discussion and lecture belong in an integrated language arts program. The teacher is not the "sage on the stage." The primary role of a teacher is to create an environment in which students are *willing* to participate orally. But how does a teacher achieve this student-driven environment for oral language?

Talking, speaking, and discussing are vital features of an English language arts classroom. However, oral communication, which is probably the most prevalent strategy for disseminating content in the English language arts classroom, is the one that teacher education programs focus on least. Teachers should be encouraged to create learning environments in which students feel invited to discuss their ideas and are prompted to solve problems through an open forum.

The good news is that we offer tips and strategies for creating effective questions and class discussions in the classroom. In addition, we show how to incorporate these strategies in class discussion, questioning, and other oral language exchanges.

To begin, if at all possible, change the setup of the classroom to make it more conducive for a class discussion. Here are some strategies and guidelines that we have gathered from our own experiences in urban and rural schools, as well as those from colleagues and former students.

Guidelines for Class Discussion

- Invite the students to ask questions. As Manny, an eighth-grade student from a large urban middle school proclaimed, "I like to ask the questions, because they're *my* questions and I think they're more interesting."
- Let students drive the discussion. They can ask the questions that stimulate class discussion, then answer their classmates' questions. As the first two items in this list indicate, the teacher needs to give up some control in order to encourage student interaction.
- Many of our students may not trust the fact that their opinions matter. It takes time to break old habits and routines. Be patient. This cannot be stressed enough. It can take an entire quarter or semester for the students to believe and trust that *their questions* and *their answers* matter the most.

LeAnn, a twenty-year veteran teacher in a large urban high school, remarked that one of her greatest teaching challenges was to "give up some of the control of the class to the students." She had been discouraged by the students' lack of enthusiasm during classroom discussions and decided that she needed to do something drastic. "We just stared at each other as I waited for them to respond to my questions."

Chapter Two

Preparing Through Pre-Reading

Although pre-reading strategies are important when studying all types of literature, they are especially crucial in helping students comprehend and unpack canonical literature. At first glance, the settings in canonical text seem alien to the everyday twenty-first-century experience, but through the use of pre-reading activities we can create windows to these worlds for our students to shape and understand their personal connections with the literature they read. By using pre-reading activities with canonical literature, we challenge our students' claims that "this book has nothing to do with me" and empower them to shape and understand their personal connections with canonical literature. Through these windows, students can develop a thematic consciousness of sorts and realize that their contemporary lives are not that different from the text world they are about to enter.

As teachers of adolescents, we sometimes overlook the importance of an effective pre-reading activity; as a result, the only way we learn is from our battle scars. We know we are guilty of this and have, in fact, learned from several instructional struggles. A primary reason for struggling readers is that, as teachers, we may not take the time to observe and assess our students' needs or to guide and assist them in entering a text world. Soon after we began doing pre-reading experiences, we witnessed firsthand how students' claims that "this book has nothing to do me" were being challenged.

Exhibit 2.1   Strategies and Skill Sets

Pre-Reading Strategy	Appropriate for These Learning Styles	Multiple Intelligences
Poster Project	Visual/Kinesthetic	Visual/Spatial Logical/Mathematical Bodily/Kinesthetic Interpersonal
Music Project	Auditory	Musical/Rhythmic Logical/Mathematical Verbal/Linguistic Intrapersonal
Shorter Works Project	Visual	Verbal/Linguistic Logical/Mathematical
Drama-as-power Project	Tactile/Kinesthetic	Bodily/Kinesthetic Interpersonal Visual/Spatial Intrapersonal
Role-Play Project	Tactile/Kinesthetic Auditory	Bodily/Kinesthetic Interpersonal Visual/Spatial Intrapersonal
Visual Arts Gallery Project	Visual	Visual/Spatial Interpersonal Musical/Rhythmic

Pre-reading activities invite students to enter a text. Exhibit 2.1 lists the pre-reading exercises covered in this chapter and the various learning styles that may be accommodated by using these strategies.

Poster Project

> You know, Ms. McKnight, those Russian serfs are no different from the homeless people who live under the train tracks two blocks from here.
>
> Urban city student comment about Russians after the Poster Project activity, prior to reading
> Russian author Chekhov's *The Cherry Orchard*

On the first day that Katie's seniors were to read *The Cherry Orchard* by Chekhov, she invited them to respond to the following prompt in their journals:

- Think of a time when something in your life changed.
- How did you handle the life change?
- Did you try to go back to "the way things used to be," or did you accept the change with little struggle? (Some life changes could include moving to a new home, changing schools, an addition to the family, a loss to your family.)

Katie thought that journal writing would support the students' comprehension, as it had done on other occasions. Her students' responses to the journal prompts supported her supposition that they comprehended the major theme of the play; however, as they began reading the play, many students lay their heads on their desks. The faces of other students displayed extreme frustration and a lack of interest. "OK, what gives?" Katie asked them. "Why the glum faces?"

"Well, Ms. McKnight, this play is *boring*. Nothing about it makes sense!" they said. Katie told them not to worry and that it would make sense to them later, so she pushed through the scene.

As they continued to read scene 1, the students kept interrupting the reading of the scene, asking Katie who this king was or who this member of the Russian royal family was. They also asked about what the conflicts were that Chekhov was referring to. As they were nearing the end of the initial scene in *The Cherry Orchard*, it dawned on Katie where her students' disconnect was coming from. Not only did they know nothing about Russian royalty and the conflicts that gave rise to the revolution of 1917, they had *no clue* about Russian history in general.

> *Self-Reflection*
> **What actions and reactions do your students demonstrate that let you know they are not relating to the material?**

Her goal, through the pre-reading strategy of journal writing, was to introduce Chekhov's major theme of the play. Katie realized that although journal writing had introduced the theme of the play, her senior students would not be able to connect with *this particular* text world if she did not provide them with the opportunity to get some background in Russian history. Katie went home that night feeling like a failure as a teacher. She had made the very assumption that she had tried for years to avoid as a teacher: *don't assume anything.*

Katie needed to regroup. She found a potential solution when she recalled a pre-reading activity that she had used successfully in a similar situation—when she taught Fitzgerald's *The Great Gatsby* to a class of sophomores. As was the case with the students studying Chekhov, this class had possessed a limited historical knowledge of the ''Roaring Twenties''—the setting and context of Fitzgerald's novel. The Poster Project that we outline in the upcoming pages provided the opportunity to build students' schema prior to reading the novel. Students chose to create posters that described various topics from the 1920s, such as prohibition, gangsters, clothes, flappers, and cars. By providing students with the opportunity to choose their own topic surrounding this time period, she gave them the opportunity to develop a personal connection with the subject matter, making the reading of this material from the 1920s relevant to their current lives.

Katie took this activity and applied it to the Chekhov novel. The assignment shown in Exhibit 2.2 was distributed to seniors on the second day of the course.

Exhibit 2.3 presents a student review form, and Exhibit 2.4 shows the rubric for the assignment.

What happened? Once her seniors received approval from their crabby editor (Katie), they spent one week researching and preparing their feature article presentations. For each student, the class became the ''editorial review board''; they discussed the proposals and what the posters revealed about Russian society at this time.

The students responded to this assignment with interest because everyone had a different topic assignment, and the writing-research partners selected the topic they wished to explore and present. The class created posters on a wide variety of topics that included

- Cosmetics
- Clothing
- Cars
- Living environments
- The Moscow subway system
- Royal palaces
- The royal family
- Food
- Famous musicians
- Religion

Through the pre-reading poster presentations, Katie's class

- Explored the difference between the social classes in Chekhov's Russia and the United States

Exhibit 2.2 Sample Poster Project Lesson

Assignment	Poster Project for *Chekov's World*
Background	Congratulations! You are an important feature writer for *Visions of History* magazine. Your crabby editor is on deadline and has demanded that you write a feature article on Russia during Anton Chekhov's time. She wants topics that are interesting for the reader, and they must be researched. Even though your editor is demanding, you're ready for the challenge and immediately go back to your writing and research partner to brainstorm topics that would be of interest to the magazine's readers. (Apparently, the crabby editor is offering bonuses for outstanding articles.)
Possible Topics	Some of the brainstormed topics include Music: Performers and trends Art: Influential artists and important trends in the art world What life is like for the average Russian living in Moscow (or other big Russian city) prior to the historic Russian Revolution of 1917 Kinds of transportation that exist today (how the average Russian "gets around" (There are dozens more that the writing team can present.)
	Once you and your writing-research partner have approval from the editor, please research the topic and prepare a poster to present at the editor's meeting. The poster should contain pictures and text showing the teacher and the editorial staff that this is a worthy topic for a feature article in the next issue.
Deadline	[*insert date*]

Exhibit 2.3 Student Review Form

Poster Presenters		Poster Topics	
Assessment Criteria		**Yes**	**No**
This presentation was well researched.			
I learned a lot from reviewing the poster.			
The poster was presented in an interesting manner.			
The poster presentation was neat and orderly.			

Exhibit 2.4 Rubric for Poster Project

✓+	Exceeds standards	My/our poster contained pictures and text that were approved by my teacher. My poster contained at least 6 to 8 entries and was arranged in a neat, easy-to-follow format. The topics on my poster were obviously researched.
✓	Meets standards	The topic of my/our poster contained pictures and text that were approved by my teacher. My poster contained at least 6 to 8 entries and was arranged in a neat, easy-to-follow format.
✓−	Does not meet standards	The topic of my poster was not approved by my teacher.

- Was amazed by the Moscow subway and shocked to learn the number of Russian soldiers who perished during World War I
- Celebrated the beauty of Russian ballet and Tchaikovsky's music

When the students were done with the presentations, the response was more positive than it had been prior to the activity.

After completing the Poster Project, Katie decorated the walls of the classroom with the visually enticing posters that the students had created, then continued with their reading of Chekhov's *The Cherry Orchard*.

"Oh!" her class jokester, Fumi, declared, "I get the stuff that was going on at the time!"

As the students continued reading the scenes, Katie took a step back and observed her students. A week after the Russian history blitz, the students were more attentive when they read certain scenes aloud in class and were not asking as many questions about the plot as prior to the poster activity.

Katie asked students to write about their experience in their journals. "I never knew about all of this," reflected one student, named Terrence. Tanisha, one of the outspoken seniors, wrote this in her journal:

I HATED this play 'cuz it was sooooooo boring. But when we did the article thing, I learned more about the people and that makes the play more interesting. I still don't like the play as much as some other stuff that we've read but it's not so bad.

Tanisha's honest and insightful reaction helped confirm what Katie had learned through observation. The honesty in student journals can be very helpful in defining which teaching strategies are working for specific students and which strategies are not.

Through this pre-reading activity, Katie provided her students the opportunity to develop a personal connection with this time period in Russian history. As a result, the students were able to build their schema on Russian history *prior* to reading; they could then enter Chekhov's story world in *The Cherry Orchard* equipped with background information. This pre-reading strategy also helped the students brush up on their research, writing, and oral presentation skills.

Through the Poster Project, the students built a bridge between their contemporary lives and a seemingly long-ago time, and discovered numerous connections between their world and Chekhov's.

Monisha's comments summed up the connections they had made using this poster pre-reading activity:

Just like us, people are left out. . . . People are discriminated against and trying to figure out how to have a good life. People are dealing with that now.

A Power Project Lesson Plan is shown in Exhibit 2.5.

Guidelines for Creating an Effective Poster Pre-Reading Activity

When creating inquiry questions for canonical text, try to create prompts that

- Are thought provoking
- Encourage students to use metacognitive strategies
- Tie in the themes of the canonical literature with personal reflection

Guidelines for Follow-Up Discussion to the Poster Project

- Ask first for general responses.
- Avoid sharing your opinion; we need to get the kids thinking.
- Focus on the students' opinions.
- Repeat what the students say to validate their reactions and elicit further reflection.

Exhibit 2.5   Poster Project Lesson Plan

Pre-Reading Mini-Lesson	Poster Project
Objective	In order to build on schema for the canonical literature they are studying, have students create a poster that relates to the time and location of the author's origin.
Materials	Poster board Magazines Scissors Markers Glue sticks Access to the library or Internet
Example	Author: Anton Chekhov Work: *The Cherry Orchard* Assignment: Have students create a poster researching information on Russia during Anton Chekhov's time. Topics might include Music: Performers and trends Art: Influential artists and trends in the art world Lifestyle: What life was like for the average Russian Transportation
Time	1 week

Procedure

Step 1	Present the assignment in the form of a request from an editor (see Exhibit 2.2).
Step 2	Students may work individually or choose a partner.
Step 3	After four days of research and preparation, students must present their poster to the class.
Step 4	This information is then compiled onto a document and circulated to all students.
IRA/NCTE Standards	**7.** Students conduct research on issues and interests by generating ideas and questions, and by posing problems. They gather, evaluate, and synthesize data from a variety of sources (e.g., print and nonprint texts, artifacts, people) to communicate their discoveries in ways that suit their purpose and audience. **8.** Students use a variety of technological and information resources (e.g., libraries, databases, computer networks, video) to gather and synthesize information and to create and communicate knowledge.

Music Project

Over fifteen years ago in her ninth-grade classroom, Katie blasted Suzanne Vega's melancholy tune, *Calypso*, over an ancient tape player. Although it was an uncomfortably hot spring day, students listened intently. After the song was over, the students sat silently, until one young girl spoke up and said, ''Can we listen to it again?'' The other students nodded their heads in agreement. At the students' request, they listened to the song twice that day, their facial and bodily expressions mirroring the mood conveyed in the song.

Little did the students know it, but Katie had used Suzanne Vega's song to sneakily guide them into the text world of their current reading—Homer's epic, the *Odyssey*. As the song came to a close, she asked the students what they thought of it and made a correlation to the novel they would be reading soon.

''She loves this guy but she lets him go and she's all alone and sad. Is the *Odyssey* all sad?'' one student asked. ''Is all of it like this?''

As Katie had hoped, the seed had been planted and the students' curiosity had been piqued. Now that the students had a sense of what was about to come next in Homer's words, the stage was set to explore this text.

Music is an outstanding pre-reading tool—an effective building block for students to develop a stance on a topic before they start reading the related text. Contemporary songs that echo the stories found in canonical literature are another pathway that leads to a connection between the times of our students and the seemingly long-ago stories.

Music as a pre-reading strategy does the following:

- Addresses the needs of auditory learners and those with musical or rhythmic intelligences
- Allows students to learn a great deal about the text before tackling the more complex language of the literature
- Allows students to envision connections between stories
- Offers thematic, mood, or other literary devices to connect to the texts
- Activates prediction and other important reading skills when listened to before reading a given text

Contemporary songs and music can unleash powerful connections to canonical literature, as students explore the themes and stories that authors present to their readers. Through the use of music as a pre-reading strategy, students learn the basic plot of the classic literature they are studying. Through the renditions by contemporary artists, they also discover that they can relate to the classic literature in a way that they weren't aware of. Songs also provide students with the opportunity to explore how the two versions of a story differ, as well as discuss the decisions that these artists made as they created their own versions of the works.

The most important question that a teacher can ask students is, ''Why did this musical artist make a musical version of this canonical text?'' Perhaps it's because the story is so interesting.

It is particularly enjoyable to bring in music that's commonly heard on the radio for pre-reading activities. To prepare for incorporating music into lessons, it is helpful to identify the radio stations that students listen to and to check these stations out during the drive to work; more than likely, there will be songs, like the one described next, that are renditions of classical pieces of literature. In addition, valuable information about students can be revealed in the songs, which can help teachers and students connect.

The Rime of the Ancient Mariner

Iron Maiden has performed a version of Coleridge's "The Rime of the Ancient Mariner" (see Exhibit 2.6), which Katie began using in her classes. Her students were often suspicious when she entered the classroom with a boom box on her shoulder and her Iron Maiden CD, ready to crank the volume for her sleepy first-period class. As the students considered the lyrics, however, they began exploring the ideas presented in Coleridge's poem.

As the students continued listening to the song, more clues were revealed. Not only were they being exposed to the basic plot of the poem and the overall

Exhibit 2.6   "The Rime of the Ancient Mariner" and Iron Maiden Lyrics

Iron Maiden's "The Rime of the Ancient Mariner" Pre-Reading Insight

Hear the rime of the ancient mariner See his eye as he stops one of three Mesmerizes one of the wedding guests Stay here and listen to the nightmares of the sea And the music plays on, as the bride passes by Caught by his spell and the mariner tells his tale.	Students can determine that the setting is at a wedding and that the ancient mariner has troublesome stories about his adventures on the sea.
Driven south to the land of the snow and the ice To a place where nobody's been Through the snow fog flies on the albatross Hailed in god's name, hoping good luck it brings. And the ship sails on, back to the north Through the fog and ice and the albatross follows on.	They know that mariner travels to colder regions of the planet and that the albatross is a bird of "good omen."

thematic messages, this heavy-metal musical interpretation also employed some of Coleridge's poetic elements.

When the musicians wrote, "And the curse goes on and on at sea / And the curse goes on and on for them and me," the lines mimic the repetitive phrases, alliteration, and assonance that Coleridge employs in his poem. As do readers of Coleridge's poem, those in Iron Maiden's audience discover the sufferings of the mariner.

Exhibit 2.7 presents several songs and lyrics that are useful for pre-reading before tackling larger works. Students will probably make many of their own contributions to this list. Exhibit 2.8 contains a pre-reading lesson plan.

Resources on the Internet for Music and Art. Here are some resources to help in gathering materials for the two previous lessons, using music and art for pre-reading:

Free Music

http://www.edu-cyberpg.com/Music/m_sites.html

Free Art

http://eduscapes.com/tap/topic98.htm

Copyright-Free Art
Large-Image Resources and Indexes
Copyright-Free Photo Archives—27,000 images from NASA, NOAA, and FWS
   http://gimp-savvy.com/PHOTO-ARCHIVE/
DHD Multimedia Gallery—Selection of images and sounds
   http://gallery.hd.org/index.jsp
Free Foto
   http://www.freefoto.com/
Free Images—2,500 stock photos (most free, some members-only)
   http://www.freeimages.co.uk/
Free Stock Photos
   http://freestockphotos.com/
Imageafter
   http://www.imageafter.com/
MorgueFile
   http://www.morguefile.com/
Pics4Learning—great for general topics
   http://pics4learning.com/
Smithsonian Institution's Office of Imaging and Photographic Services
   http://photo2.si.edu/

Photo Resources
ARS (Agricultural Research Service) Image Gallery
   http://www.ars.usda.gov/is/graphics/photos/
Art Images for College Teaching
   http://arthist.cla.umn.edu/aict/index.html

Exhibit 2.7 Canonical Text and Related Music

Author	Text	Song Title/ Artist
Edwin Arlington Robinson	"Richard Cory"	"Richard Cory" by Wings
Maya Angelou	*I Know Why the Caged Bird Sings*	"Caged Bird" by Alicia Keys
Emily Bronte	*Wuthering Heights*	"Wuthering Heights" by Kate Bush
Samuel Taylor Coleridge	"Kubla Khan"	"Xanadu" by Rush
Samuel Taylor Coleridge	"The Rime of the Ancient Mariner"	"The Rime of the Ancient Mariner" by Iron Maiden
Dante	"The Inferno"	"Dante's Prayer" by Lorena McKennitt
John Donne	Poems by John Donne	"Rave on John Donne" by Van Morrison
Nathaniel Hawthorne	"Young Goodman Brown"	"Shohhoth's Old Peculiar" by The Kindly Ones
Homer	*The Odyssey*	"Tales of Brave Ulysses" by Cream "Home at Last" by Steely Dan "Lotus Eaters" by Moloko
Aldus Huxley	*Brave New World*	"Brave New World" by Iron Maiden
John Milton	"Paradise Lost"	"Song of Joy" by Nick Caves
George Orwell	*1984*	"1984" by David Bowie
Edgar Allan Poe	"Cask of Amontillado"	"Cask of Amontillado" by Alan Parsons Project
Edgar Allan Poe	"Lady Legeia"	"Vanishing Act" by Lou Reed

Exhibit 2.7 *(continued)*

Author	Text	Song Title/ Artist
Edgar Allan Poe	"Murders in the Rue Morgue"	"Murders in the Rue Morgue" by Iron Maiden
William Shakespeare	*Romeo and Juliet*	"Romeo and Juliet by Dire Straits "Romeo and Juliet" by Indigo Girls "Kissing You" by Des'ree
William Shakespeare	"Tempest"	"Prospero's Speech" by Lorena McKennitt
William Shakespeare	"Sonnet 142"	"The Miseducation of Lauryn Hill" by Lauryn Hill
Sophocles	"Oedipus Rex"	"Oedipus Rex" by Tom Lehrer
Alfred Lord Tennyson	"The Lady of Shallot"	"Left Me a Fool" by Indigo Girls
J.R.R. Tolkien	*The Lord of the Rings*	"Ramble On" by Led Zeppelin
Mark Twain	*The Adventures of Huckleberry Finn*	"Barefoot Children in the Rain" by Jimmy Buffet
Mark Twain	*The Adventures of Tom Sawyer*	"Tom Sawyer" by Rush
William Wordsworth	The Lucy Poems	"Lucy" by The Divine Comedy
W. B. Yeats	"Before the World Was Made"	"Mofo" by U2

Exhibit 2.8   Music Pre-Reading Lesson Plan

Pre-Reading Lesson	**Music as a Pre-Reading Strategy**
Objective	To develop connections between contemporary popular culture and canonical literature. To offer thematic, mood, or other connective literary devices.
Materials	Musical device (CD player, tape player, or computer)
Example	Author: Homer Work: *The Odyssey* Related Music: Suzanne Vega's "Calypso" Assignment: Have students listen to music before reading a story.
Time	One to two class periods

Procedure	
Step 1	Choose a contemporary song that relates to the canonical literature you are working with.
Step 2	Play the song twice for the students.
Step 3	Have a classroom discussion about the song. Questions could include What was the song about? What did you think of the song? Why do you think this artist chose this song?
Step 4	Relate the song to the text you are working with.
IRA/NCTE Standards	**3.** Students apply a wide range of strategies to comprehend, interpret, evaluate, and appreciate texts. They draw on their prior experience, their interactions with other readers and writers, their knowledge of word meaning and of other texts, their word identification strategies, and their understanding of textual features (e.g., sound-letter correspondence, sentence structure, context, graphics). **11.** Students participate as knowledgeable, reflective, creative, and critical members of a variety of literacy communities.

Free Public Domain (PD) Images—small collection
   http://www.pdimages.com/web6.htm
Great Images in NASA
   http://grin.hq.nasa.gov/
JSC Digital Image Collection (NASA)—search or browse 9,000 NASA images
   http://images.jsc.nasa.gov/
NASA Multimedia Gallery—images, video, and interactive features
   http://www.nasa.gov/multimedia/highlights/index.html
Natural Resources Conservation Service (NRCS) Photo Gallery
   http://photogallery.nrcs.usda.gov/
NOAA (National Oceanic and Atmospheric Administration) Photo Library
   —search 20,000 NOAA images
   http://www.photolib.noaa.gov/
Planetary Photojournalfrom NASA
   http://photojournal.jpl.nasa.gov/
Public Health Image Library (PHIL) from Centers for Disease Control and
   Prevention
   http://phil.cdc.gov/Phil/default.asp
U.S. Fish and Wildlife Service: Pictures/Graphics
   http://pictures.fws.gov/

Images on Specific Topics
Abraham Lincoln—5 pictures
   http://showcase.netins.net/web/creative/lincoln/resource/freepix.htm
Images from the History of Medicine (IHM) from National Library of
   Medicine
   http://wwwihm.nlm.nih.gov/
Images of American Political History
   http://teachpol.tcnj.edu/amer_pol_hist/
Map Collections: 1500–2003 from *American Memory*, Library of Congress
   http://memory.loc.gov/ammem/gmdhtml/gmdhome.html
Moving Image Archive from *Internet Archive*
   http://www.archive.org/movies/movies.php

Text Resources
Project Gutenberg(electronic texts)
   http://gutenberg.net/
Stories and Characters That Have Had Their Copyright Expire
   http://www.pdimages.com/stories.htm

Music
Links to Search for PD Music and Lyrics
   http://www.pdinfo.com/link.htm (not completely free and have some
   restrictions; see the site for further information.)
American Memory from the Library of Congress
   http://rs6.loc.gov/amhome.html
Free Photographs
   http://www.free-photographs.net/

Stockphoto
http://www.istockphoto.com/
Metropolitan Museum of Art, New York
http://www.metmuseum.org/home.asp
NASA Image eXchange (NIX)
http://nix.nasa.gov/
New York Public Library Picture Collection Online
http://digital.nypl.org/mmpco/ Collection of 30,000 digitized images from books, magazines, and newspapers, as well as original photographs, prints, and postcards, mostly created before 1923.

Caveats regarding the use of music and images: (1) fair use of these images for education and research is permissible; (2) avoid using trademarked images like those from Disney or other large media outlets.

Shorter Works Project

Before her class read *The Crucible* (Arthur Miller's play that examines the hysteria caused by the Salem Witch Trials), Katie and her students examined the actual court records from the trials. After the students had taken some time to read over the documents and journal briefly about what they thought, Katie opened up the floor for a class discussion.

"Man, people just go off on each other don't they? What's wrong with them?" one sophomore replied. Through the students' examination of the actual Salem Witch Trial court documents, they came to understand that Miller's play is based on actual events that took place over four hundred years ago. Even more important, Katie explained that the catalyst for Miller to write *The Crucible* (about the Salem witch trials) was the McCarthy hearings, an event that occurred a mere fifty years ago.

Having students read a shorter work that echoes the themes and story of a longer canonical work can be quite helpful as a pre-reading strategy. "Readers may apply to their reading what they know about the attitudes and values or 'ethos' of a particular historical period" (Beach and Marshall, 1990, p. 260). Historical and background information can aid students' understanding of and engagement with the text. With this kind of background information, students may consider and process different interpretations or explanations of a text.

Through classroom discussion, the students also explored contemporary examples of times when public events become polarizing issues for the current society. Students addressed the corruptive influence of a few in a larger society through the McCarthy hearings and, in later years, the demise of corporate giants like Enron and MCI World Com. In addition, they discussed the polarizing issues of the particular time they were in—the involvement of President Clinton and his wife, Hillary, in the Whitewater scandal or the O. J. Simpson trial and the effect that groups can have on public opinion. They knew, from these present-day examples, that the events during the Salem Witch Trials were not isolated.

By applying historical and biographical information, students do more than simply recall facts; through these shorter works, they begin to see how a small group can create hysteria among a larger group of largely sensible individuals. They are exposed to the powers of manipulation and hysteria.

Exhibit 2.9 contains some short works that can be used as pre-reading for larger classical texts. Exhibit 2.10 contains a pre-reading lesson.

As Figure 2.1 demonstrates, shorter and longer works can be connected thematically. These connecting themes bridge meaningful connections between readers and texts. Once students make the thematic connections between texts, they are equipped to become more reflective in their reading and can offer comments like "I know from reading this that . . ." and "Questions I have from reading this are . . ."

Exhibit 2.9   Related Sample Short Works for Canonical Literature

Canonical Literature Title and Author	Sample Related Short Work and Author
"Beowulf"	"The Man Who Came Too Early" by Poul Anderson (contemporary science fiction story) "The Seafarer" (Anglo-Saxon poem)
The Crucible by Arthur Miller	Salem Court Documents (court records) Senator McCarthy Hearings (congressional documents)
The Scarlet Letter by Nathaniel Hawthorne	"Young Goodman Brown" by Nathaniel Hawthorne (short story)
I Know Why the Caged Bird Sings by Maya Angelou	"Sympathy" by Paul Laurence Dunbar (poem)
All Quiet on the Western Front by Erich Maria Remarque or *A Farewell to Arms* by Ernest Hemingway	"Death Be Not Proud" by John Donne "A Mother's Lament for the Death of Her Son" by Robert Burns "Death Is a Dialogue" by Emily Dickinson
The Time Machine and *War of the Worlds* by H. G. Wells	"Time Long Past" by Percy Bysshe Shelley

Teaching the Classics in the Inclusive Classroom

Exhibit 2.10 Shorter Works Pre-Reading Lesson

Pre-Reading Lesson	Shorter Works As a Bridge
Objective	Create an atmosphere by pre-reading shorter works where students can potentially connect with different text worlds. This is key in creating effective pre-reading strategies.
Materials	Shorter works related to the canonical literature being studied
Time	45 minutes

Procedure	
Step 1	Pass out a copy of the related shorter work to each student.
Step 2	After students read these copies, place the students into groups to discuss the shorter works.
Step 3	Ask the students the following questions: What did you think of these documents? What other issues from our time reflect these same sentiments?
IRA/NCTE Standards	1. Students read a wide range of print and non-print texts to build an understanding of texts, of themselves, and of the cultures of the United States and the world; to acquire new information; to respond to the needs and demands of society and the workplace; and for personal fulfillment. Among these texts are fiction and nonfiction, classic, and contemporary works.

2. Students read a wide range of literature from many periods in many genres to build an understanding of the many dimensions (e.g., philosophical, ethical, aesthetic) of human experience.

3. Students apply a wide range of strategies to comprehend, interpret, evaluate, and appreciate texts. They draw on their prior experience, their interactions with other readers and writers, their knowledge of word meaning and of other texts, their word identification strategies, and their understanding of textual features (e.g., sound-letter correspondence, sentence structure, context, graphics). |

Figure 2.1   Connecting Text Worlds

Title of First Shorter Literary Work _____	
I know from reading this that…	Questions I have from reading this are:

Title of Second Shorter Literary Work _____	
I know from reading this that…	Questions I have from reading this are:

Connecting themes of Literary Work _____	
I know from reading this that…	Questions I have from reading this are:

Teaching the Classics in the Inclusive Classroom

National-Louis University Library

presents...

Katherine S. McKnight, PHD and Mary Scruggs's new book...

The Second City
Guide to
Improv in the Classroom
Using Improvisation to Teach Skills and Boost Learning

This book is the result of the educational programming offered by The Second City Training Centers in Chicago and Toronto. The ready-to-use exercises in this book are used to teach a variety of subjects—including literacy, math, science, and social studies—and builds classroom community and develops cooperative learning skills. **Katherine S. McKnight, PhD**, is an Associate Professor at National-Louis University and an onsite consultant for the National Council of Teachers of English. **Mary Scruggs** is Head of Writing and Education Programs at The Second City Training Centers in Chicago.

Two Presentations!!

NLU North Shore Campus	**NLU Chicago Campus**
Thursday, October 2, 2008	Wednesday, October 22, 2008
4:00pm - Public Forum Room #353	4:00pm - Room #5012 A&B
5202 Old Orchard Road, Skokie	122 S. Michigan Avenue, Chicago

Refreshments will be served!

RSVP not required but greatly appreciated Libevents@nl.edu

Hosted by the NLU Library Outreach Committee

Drama-as-Power Project

There are other, perhaps untraditional, methods for engagement that facilitate a student's personal connection with literature. Rosenblatt (1978) asserts that "the benefits of literature can emerge only from creative activity on the part of the reader himself" (p. 276). Like drama, reading for meaning and exploration demands the reader's involvement and participation in the text.

The connection between reading literature and drama is described by Rosenblatt (1978):

> We accept the fact that the actor infuses his own voice, his own body, his own gestures—in short, his own interpretation—into the words of the text. Is he not carrying to its ultimate manifestations what each of us as readers of text must do? (p. 13).

Like actors, when we are engaged as readers, we allow ourselves to participate in the imaginary text worlds. Reading literature, according to Rosenblatt (1995), is the reader's participation in a "transaction" with text that produces meaning.

For less engaged readers, who tend to have the most difficulty reading challenging literature such as the canon, creative dramatics can aid their understanding of the text.

The act of reading is described as the creation of "secondary worlds" and the involvement and enactment of drama within these text worlds (Britton, 1970). If readers are placed into this secondary world through creative dramatics, then they are experiencing and reacting to the text from within. This kind of participant stance that the reader takes allows him or her to participate in this text world rather than be a spectator.

Thinking of methods and strategies that catapult a student into the text is a primary goal for teaching literature. How can we help students visualize and experience the texts they read? Visualizing text through creative dramatics can nurture their engagement with text.

As a pre-reading activity, drama strategies do the following:

- Aid disengaged readers in the understanding of the canonical text
- Address the needs of the kinesthetic learner
- Allow students to evoke and exert control over the ideas, sensations, characters, and meanings
- Allow students to participate in the text world rather than be passive spectators

A strategy that Katie learned at the National Endowment for the Humanities Shakespeare Institute exposes students to major themes in *Hamlet* before they even crack the binding of the play. She says, ''I have often found that students skim over lengthy passages where one character is the primary speaker.'' What students often don't realize is that important plot elements and insights into the characters are in these passages.

This is particularly characteristic of Shakespeare's monologues and soliloquies, such as Hamlet's ''To Be or Not to Be'' speech at the beginning of the play. This speech offers some important insights into the title character and foreshadows key conflicts and plot elements.

Drama strategies, such as the exercise provided in Exhibit 2.11, can slow down students' reading speed so they can focus on what the character is saying.

What happens? The students soon discover that Hamlet is very unhappy and is contemplating suicide. Before they begin the text, they already know the title character's main conflict in act 1 and are already considering sources for his unhappiness. They are using their reading skills, too, as they make predictions about possible events in the play.

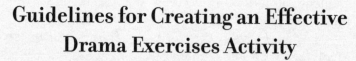

Guidelines for Creating an Effective Drama Exercises Activity

Create inquiry questions for canonical text to create prompts, which should be

- Thought provoking and should tie the themes of the canonical literature with personal reflection
- Predict character actions and potential consequences of those actions
- Synthesize moral character conflicts with present or real-life situations

Guidelines for Follow-Up Discussion to Drama Exercises

- Ask for general responses first.
- Avoid sharing your opinion.
- Focus on the students' opinions and repeat what they say, in order to elicit further reflection.
- Encourage and model active questioning (*example:* "If Macbeth didn't kill Duncan, what would have happened?")

Exhibit 2.11   Drama-as-Power Lesson Plan

Pre-Reading Lesson	Drama as Power
Educational Benefit	Active exploration and manipulation of text
Example	Hamlet's "To Be or Not to Be" speech from William Shakespeare's play, *Hamlet*
Materials	Index cards, each one with a line from a monologue from the play.
Time	15–20 minutes

Preparation

Step 1	Identify the purpose for your pre-reading activity: What information are you looking for the students to learn from the activity? What issues do you want to clarify in the activity? Character motivation? Character conflict? Themes? Choose a monologue that conveys the information that students need to learn.
Step 2	Write each line of this monologue on a separate index card.

Procedure

Step 1	Arrange the students in a circle.
Step 2	Hand each student a card with a line from the text, keeping the lines in sequence as you distribute the cards.
Step 3	In a circle, each student will act the line of the text.
Step 4	Have the group of students practice their lines of the monologues as a group a couple of times. These practice sessions can provide students with additional time to reflect on the text being read.
Step 5	The ultimate goal is to make it sound like one person is speaking.

Follow-up Discussion to Drama Pre-reading Strategy

IRA/NCTE Standards	2. Students read a wide range of literature from many periods in many genres to build an understanding of the many dimensions (e.g., philosophical, ethical, aesthetic) of human experience.
	3. Students apply a wide range of strategies to comprehend, interpret, evaluate, and appreciate texts. They draw on their prior experience, their interactions with other readers and writers, their knowledge of word meaning and of other texts, their word identification strategies, and their understanding of textual features (e.g., sound-letter correspondence, sentence structure, context, graphics).

Role-Play Project

Katie first discovered the power of creative dramatics for teaching English when she attended a National Endowment for the Humanities Institute for Teaching Shakespeare over ten years ago. There she learned how to unleash the humanity of written text through instructional drama-based activities.

Her juniors always read "The Pardoner's Tale" from Chaucer's masterpiece, *The Canterbury Tales.* "The Pardoner's Tale" focuses on the story of three rioters who are prompted to "find death." As the rioters search for death, they find riches near a tree and soon plot against each other as a means to claim the riches for themselves. Eventually, they do "find death" by killing each other over the treasure from the tree.

As a pre-reading activity, Katie used her training to invite the students to create a role-play or skit in which they and their fellow performers look for death. During the role-play, each group of students needed to indicate to the audience what "death" might be. Over the years of using this pre-reading strategy, Katie has seen at least fifty versions of this skit in her classroom. The most common form the students role-played was death due to some illegal drug—an interesting statement on contemporary society. Through the use of role-playing a dramatic activity, her students, like Chaucer, became social commentators and were able to connect with the text by relating the theme to present-day situations.

Another example of a theme Katie used was the scenario "Is it ever OK to steal?"—one of the primary themes in *Les Miserables.*

Before the students read a text, take a basic theme from the canonical work or from a few of the chapters and instruct students to create a situation in which they reenact that same theme. Then have the students enact the scenes for their classmates.

When the students have completed their role-plays or skits, have a large-group discussion about the themes and ideas that were presented by the different groups. As the students share their thoughts and feelings, bridge their presentations to the text that the class is about to read. Through this activity, the students develop a sense of what the text is about and are predisposed to discover how the text will unfold the text.

> **Self-Reflection**
> What is the primary theme of the canonical book that your students are currently reading? Does your class contain students who are more kinesthetic learners, who may become engaged in a role-playing activity?

As a pre-reading strategy, role-playing does the following:

- Addresses the needs of students with Bodily/Kinesthetic Intelligence, Visual/Spatial Intelligence, and Interpersonal Intelligence

- Allows the teacher to develop connections to canonical works through auditory, visual, and kinesthetic learning styles
- Empowers students to develop a personal connection with the text
- Exposes students to the major plot points of the related text
- Bridges a connection between drama role-playing and the canonical text

Exhibit 2.12 shows a pre-reading lesson plan for using dramatic performance. Exhibit 2.13 contains the rubric for the lesson plan. Role playing and

Exhibit 2.12   Role Playing Pre-Reading Lesson Plan

Pre-Reading Lesson	Role-Play
Objective	To use role playing and dramatic performance as a tool to develop a personal connection with canonical text as well as an understanding of the themes and major plots of canonical text.
Materials	None necessary
Time	One to two class periods
Procedure	
Step 1	Before the students read a text, take a basic theme from the canonical work or from a few of the chapters and instruct students to create a situation in which they reenact that same theme.
Step 2	Have the students enact the scenes for their classmates.
Step 3	Conduct a large-group discussion about the themes and ideas that were presented by the different student groups. Connect the information that the students presented in their presentations to the text that they're about to read.
IRA/NCTE Standards	**3.** Students apply a wide range of strategies to comprehend, interpret, evaluate, and appreciate texts. They draw on their prior experience, their interactions with other readers and writers, their knowledge of word meaning and of other texts, their word identification strategies, and their understanding of textual features (e.g., sound-letter correspondence, sentence structure, context, and graphics).
	12. Students use spoken, written, and visual language to accomplish their own purposes (e.g., for learning, enjoyment, persuasion, and the exchange of information).

Exhibit 2.13   Rubric for Role-Playing Pre-Reading Lesson Plan

✓+	Exceeds standards	Student has demonstrated a strong understanding of the theme through the creative output of the role-play. The role-play is creative and demonstrates originality.
✓	Meets Standards	The role-play demonstrates the student's understanding and interpretation of the theme/topic.
✓–	Does not meet standards	The role-play does not demonstrate the student's understanding or interpretation of the topic.

other classroom drama activities are useful tools for all types of readers but particularly for the struggling reader. These readers have the most difficulty comprehending a text, and drama activities like role playing provide the opportunity for these readers to directly enter the text world. In contrast to the text world that can create confusion and stress for some readers, the role play is a more inviting entrance. Students are given the opportunity to experience and react to the text from within.

Visual Arts Gallery Project

That really bugged me. I know why Dr. King wrote what he did.

A student reacting to pictures from the 1960s civil rights movement prior to reading "A Letter from Birmingham Jail" by Martin Luther King Jr.

A visualization of a textual world provides students with the opportunity to experience and think about a text.

Using visual arts as a pre-reading strategy does the following:

- Provides opportunities for introverted students to visualize an imaginative text world
- Helps reluctant readers enter texts and respond
- Allows students to visualize the events that are reflected in the text being studied
- Addresses the needs of visual learners

Visual art, as in the case of drama, helps reluctant readers enter texts and respond to them. Teachers are able to open their notions of reading, as well as strategies for reading. Art and drama both reinforce the necessity of drawing on the reader's prior experience to create meaning. Art also encourages students to explore and create new understanding and is a means through which to imagine and enter into text worlds (see Wilhelm, 1997).

During the Clinton administration and the 1998 U.S. military strike against Iraq, Katie was working on an assignment for a class in graduate school and observed a peer's (Jill's) English class for two weeks. Jill was a veteran English teacher, who often taught the lower-level students who were tracked into the "support" classes. She was passionate about developing the students' literacy skills so they could become "citizens of our community." During this two-week period, Jill prepared the students to read Martin Luther King Jr.'s "A Letter from Birmingham Jail," which was required reading in the ninth-grade English curriculum.

Case Example: Visual Art in the Classroom

Jill enthusiastically introduced students to the history of the civil rights movement in America:

> If we go through the experience, we know more about it and feel something about it. I remember the civil rights movement. I remember this, and this is personal for me because I lived through it. You [gesturing to her students] know something about it through books and, for some, your older relatives may have told you about it. This [Jill holds up her copy of "A Letter from Birmingham Jail"] is King's response to "man's inhumanity to man." Now, you can see that I have some pictures on the wall there and I'd like to invite you to look at my art gallery.

Jill's "art gallery" was composed of a collection of photos from books and magazines that she displayed on the classroom walls. As the students entered Jill's art gallery, they explored the historical background and impact of the civil rights movement. While perusing the pictures, one of the students hummed the famous civil rights anthem, "We Shall Overcome." Hearing the student, Jill promised to bring a recording of the song. One of the students, Walter, focused on a picture of protesters being sprayed by water hoses and asked, "Why were the water hoses such a big deal?"

"The water hoses were very painful," Jill responded. "The force of the water was so great, it could knock you down."

Jill's response seemed to satisfy Walter's curiosity, so Jill continued her civil rights mini-lesson.

"You do know," Jill shared thoughtfully, "that many non-blacks participated in the civil rights movement and lost their lives."

"Is this the bus boycott?" Marty asked, pointing to a picture.

"Yes," Jill responded. She paused. "You do know about Rosa Parks. She was the test case," she said. "When she was arrested, that started the bus boycott. As a matter of fact, the leaders of the movement were surprised that the blacks would organize so quickly. Most of the blacks didn't use buses. They organized car pools and taxis; many people walked ten to fifteen miles a day."

"Did King make any money from this?" Kim asked.

"No," Jill said. She paused as she thought about how to respond to that question. Just share the facts, she thought. "He did have a salary as a minister but if you're asking if he made a lot of money, well . . ."

Jill paused again. "The answer is no."

58

This discussion typified the progression of this pre-reading activity. While Jill directed the students through the art gallery, she allowed them to freely ask questions about the pictures and the civil rights movement.

Katie asked Jill about her decision to engage her students in this pre-reading activity. "The art gallery is a tool for the students to visualize the events that Martin Luther King Jr. discusses in his letter," Jill shared with Katie. "Many of them need to 'see' what they'll read. It seems to help them understand the material more."

After going through the art gallery, Jill had the students return to their seats and read the letter together. During the reading, Jill and the students frequently referred to the pictures and events discussed in the art-gallery tour. Among these concepts was the power of nonviolence and its consequent personal sacrifices. Two students expressed their amazement at the sacrifices that Dr. King had made during the movement. It seemed that the powerful images that Jill presented to her students affected their responses to King's letter. The following day, Jill opened a classroom discussion about the work of the day before.

"What did you think of the pictures we saw yesterday?" Jill asked.

"They were nice." Marcia responded.

Without skipping a beat, Jill pressed Marcia's response for further reflection. "That doesn't tell us anything. What impressed you?" She paused, giving the students time to reflect on the experience.

After a short period of time, a student raised his hand. "OK," she said. "Fred?"

Fred paused as he formulated his thoughts. "Good." He paused again. "They were informative."

"OK." Jill reflected back what Fred had said. "They were informative. What did you learn from the pictures?" she asked.

"It touched," Fred paused again. "Well, I was touched by them. I learned that there were female KKK members." Fred paused as he thought about the photos. "I didn't realize that there were people watching as they lynched people."

"They often watched and even laughed." Jill shared, matter-of-factly.

"That really bugged me." Fred reacted. "I know why King wrote what he did," Fred said, as he related his emotional reaction to the events he saw portrayed in the photos. "It was awful but he stayed positive." He paused as the impact of the events hit him. "I don't know if I could do that."

As the impact of Fred's statement was felt by the other students, more students became involved in the discussion, sharing examples of what they had learned from the visual art gallery and reading of "A Letter from Birmingham Jail."

"I didn't know that there were nuns involved," Abby said.

"Yes," Jill followed up. "And there were many Jews and Catholics. Did you know that there were as many non-blacks as blacks involved?"

The din of student chatter broke out in the classroom, as half the students spontaneously turned to classmates, reacting to this information. As the discussion ensued, Jill directed the discussion to the role of individual conscience.

In addition, she asked the students to compare the discrimination of the 1990s to the 1960s. As they were about to conclude this discussion and pre-reading activity, a student posed one final question for Jill.

"Do you feel that President Clinton should be concerned about our country rather than what was happening in Iraq?"

Jill directed her response to parallel the text they were studying. "Isn't there a similar pattern here? Hussein is a man who wants to stay in power and refuses to let go. He wants to stay in power at any cost. Well, isn't this what Dr. King and many others are struggling against? I mean, this is how it all started. The civil rights movement started because those who were in power didn't want to give it up, even though many people were suffering. Dr. King says it in his letter [quotes from the text]. 'Someone refuses to give up power.'"

A hush fell over the class, as the students contemplated the correlation she had made between the events unfolding in their current history and those of the text they were studying.

Through the use of the visual arts gallery, reflective classroom discussion, and the relation to current historical events, Jill had promoted the idea that an apparently simple text, such as King's letter, held many historical, contemporary, and personal layers. During this two-day pre-reading activity, Jill had helped her students to uncover these layers, introducing possible themes and conflicts to prepare them for a more thorough reading of the text.

Jill's photo gallery is just one example of how the use of visual arts and discussion can trigger students' abilities to imagine and envision a text.

Guidelines for Creating a Visual Arts Gallery

Consider the following questions as you prepare your own visual arts lesson:

What connections do you want to elicit from your students?

What photos, artwork, or film media can help students develop a personal connection with the text?

What classroom discussion can be prompted through these visual arts?

Exhibit 2.14 contains a lesson plan for use with the pre-reading visual arts activity.

Exhibit 2.14 Visual Arts Pre-Reading Lesson Plan

Pre-Reading Lesson	Visual Arts
Objective	To create a bridge between the text and the visual medium
Materials	Pictures, paintings, movies related to the canonical text being studied
Time	One to two class periods
Procedure	
Step 1	Hang pictures and paintings in the form of an art gallery.
Step 2	Invite students to browse the art gallery.
Step 3	Through a large-group discussion, elicit students' experiences as they look at the visual arts provided. Bridge the gap between the visual arts and the related text.
IRA/NCTE Standards	**1.** Students read a wide range of print and non-print texts to build an understanding of texts, of themselves, and of the cultures of the United States and the world; to acquire new information; to respond to the needs and demands of society and the workplace; and for personal fulfillment. Among these texts are fiction and nonfiction, classic, and contemporary works. **3.** Students apply a wide range of strategies to comprehend, interpret, evaluate, and appreciate texts. They draw on their prior experience, their interactions with other readers and writers, their knowledge of word meaning and of other texts, their word identification strategies, and their understanding of textual features (e.g., sound-letter correspondence, sentence structure, context, graphics).

Resources for All Pre-Reading Projects

Picture Books

Picture books provide students with a visual and auditory representation of the text they will be reading. Because of the simplicity of language and the superior artwork of many picture books nowadays, reading picture books with text related to the theme of canonical literature can provide students with an initial understanding of the theme of the text before starting to read the classic. Using picture books can also provide your classroom with a bridge for auditory and visual learners.

As a graduate student and full-time classroom teacher, Katie thought her professors were nuts when they advocated the use of picture books in a high school classroom. She thought the students would laugh her to the curb of the street if she used picture books in her classroom. Once Katie heard the message over a half a dozen times or so, she decided that she would try it.

Following is a list of picture books that Katie found helpful to use as a pre-reading strategy:

DK Books. (2000a). New York: DK Publishing.

Eyewitness Books. (2000b). New York: Children's Press (CT).

Adams, S. (2005). *The outcast who became England's queen.* Washington, D.C.: National Geographic Society.

Davidson, R. P. (2003). *All the world's a stage.* New York: Greenwillow Books.

Hopkinson, D. (2005). *Saving strawberry farm.* New York: Greenwillow Books.

Mannis, C. A. (2003). *The queen's progress.* New York: Viking Books.

Miller, W. (2001). *Rent party jazz.* New York: Lee & Low Books.

Peacock, C. A. (2004). *Pilgrim cat.* Morton Grove: Albert Whitman & Company.

Shange, N. (2004). *Ellington was not a street.* New York: Simon & Schuster Children's Publishing.

Williams, M. (1998). *Tales from Shakespeare.* Cambridge: Candlewick Press.

Anticipation Guides

Katie first used anticipation guides after her attendance at a mandatory professional development session during her first year of teaching. Reading specialists from the district where she taught explained the merits of anticipation guides.

In a nutshell, anticipation guides are great pre-reading tools for the following reasons:

- They *preview* key themes and ideas that will be presented in the upcoming text.
- They provide opportunities for students to draw on their prior knowledge and experiences, or schema.
- Students have the opportunity through anticipation guides to recognize the effects of their point of view in formulating their opinions of the text.
- Student comprehension of a selected text can be increased because of what the guides accomplish.

Katie soon discovered that anticipation guides aid students in understanding the linguistically complex text that is commonly found in the classics.

Here are some tips for the creation of an anticipation guide, as well as a sample guide.

Tips

- Create statements that relate to the text that the students are about to read. These statements could be about the themes, ideas, and characters that will be presented in the text. Generally, ten statements are manageable for the students in an anticipation guide.
- The students choose either *agree* or *disagree* after each statement.

- When good readers pick up a text, they generally anticipate what the reading will be about. However, struggling readers do not generally anticipate when they read, and the anticipation guide can help them develop this skill. Remember this as you prepare anticipation guides for your students.

The statements appear in Exhibit 2.15, and a generic template is shown in Exhibit 2.16.

When Katie's students used the anticipation guides, they reported to her that they had a better sense of what the text was about. They said that it was easier to understand the text because they knew what it was about before they read it. An eleventh-grade student, Van, whose first language was not English, said, "I like the anticipation guides because when I know what the story might be about, it is much easier for me to understand Shakespeare's language."

Exhibit 2.15   Anticipation Guide for Shakespeare's *Macbeth*

Sample Anticipation Guide

Anticipation Guide for Shakespeare's Macbeth

Directions: In the space before each statement, put an "X" to indicate whether you agree or disagree with the statements that follow. Be prepared to defend your response with specific details and explanation. Once you have read the text, go back and reevaluate your response to the statements.

Agree	Disagree	Statement
		1. Power generally corrupts those who possess it.
		2. Ambition is a good thing.
		3. A person's immoral choices always come back to haunt the person.
		4. Having the ambition to achieve a personal goal is honorable.
		5. Physical courage is easier to achieve than moral courage.
		6. Seeking revenge is sometimes necessary to gain justice.
		7. Evil breeds even more evil.
		8. Lying is OK sometimes.
		9. Eventually, justice always prevails.
		10. Family members generally take care of each other at difficult times.

Exhibit 2.16   Anticipation Guide Template

Name:
Period:

Anticipation Guide
Title:

Agree	Disagree	Statement
		1.
		2.
		3.
		4.
		5.
		6.
		7.
		8.
		9.
		10.

Pre-reading activities have the great potential to develop struggling readers' skills so that they can better comprehend and understand difficult text. In the next chapter, we will continue to present lessons, strategies, and ideas for students *during* the reading of the literature classics.

Chapter Three

During-Reading Activities

Using examples from canonical literature, this section includes reader-response lessons that promote personal response and student engagement with literature.

The following literary works are featured in this chapter:

The Epic of Gilgamesh, an epic poem from Babylonia
Romeo and Juliet by William Shakespeare
The Scarlet Letter by Nathaniel Hawthorne
The Odyssey by Homer
King Arthur and the Knights of the Round Table

Exhibit 3.1 lists the during-reading exercises covered in this chapter and the various learning styles that may be accommodated through the use of these strategies.

Exhibit 3.1   Strategies and Skill Sets

During-Reading Strategy	Appropriate for These Learning Styles	Multiple Intelligences
Making Text Kinesthetic	Tactile/Kinesthetic	Verbal/Linguistic Logical/Mathematical
Creating Graphic Novels	Tactile/Kinesthetic Visual	Bodily/Kinesthetic Interpersonal Visual/Spatial Intrapersonal
Reader's Theater	Tactile/Kinesthetic	Bodily/Kinesthetic Interpersonal Visual/Spatial Intrapersonal
Character Bookmarks	Visual	Visual/Spatial Interpersonal
Found Poetry	Tactile/Kinesthetic Visual	Visual/Spatial Verbal/Linguistic Bodily/Kinesthetic Interpersonal Musical/Rhythmic

Making Text Kinesthetic

When Brad was a student teacher in a high school where the majority of the students did not speak English as their first language, he soon discovered that his struggling readers could not visualize the text that they were reading. He asked them, after reading *The Epic of Gilgamesh*, what the title character looked like. José, a sixteen-year-old latino student, looked at him and replied, "Hey Mr. B, I have no idea what he looks like." Katie has similar teaching stories, as we are sure that readers of this book do. The question in dealing with struggling readers like José is, How do we help them visualize the text? We know that this is key to comprehending text and that it is critical for students who are reading linguistically complex literature that characteristically embodies the literature canon. One strategy for helping students visualize text is to "physicalize" the words on the page. If the students have a kinesthetic experience with the text, they are more likely to understand it.

The Story Behind the Lesson

For example, in Brad's twelfth-grade English class, as they read *The Epic of Gilgamesh*, the students had difficulty remembering the complex names found in this text. Brad assigned each character a sound and action. As a result of this pedagogical application, the students became more motivated and interested in reading the text.

By using kinesthetic strategies such as these, we can increase our students' interest level, as well as provide them with an opportunity to relate further to the text through active participation (see Exhibit 3.2).

The student-created sample script in Exhibit 3.3 can be used in your classroom. As mentioned previously, dramatic activities like this interactive reading create opportunities for struggling readers that are inviting. Every student can play some role, whether it's creating the assigned sound for each character or reading a major part. All of the students are involved. It's also helpful for literary works like *The Epic of Gilgamesh* to introduce and provide a strategy for tracking the numerous characters. (The upcoming character bookmarks discussed in this book are a perfect example of a character tracking strategy.)

Walt Whitman's "A Noiseless Patient Spider"

It's ironic that teenagers who are rebellious challengers of authority would find the American transcendentalists like Emerson, Thoreau, and, arguably, Walt Whitman so challenging to understand. For sophomores in Katie's English class this was a battle. She had to figure out how to connect the text to the students' personal lives and help them understand the very strong transcendental message of how the individual fits into the larger whole. This is a pretty important message for most sophomores but also key in understanding the messages in transcendental literature.

Exhibit 3.2   Making Text Kinesthetic Lesson Plan

During-Reading Lesson	**Keeping Track of Who's Who**
Objective	To enhance the student's ability to identify and connect to characters in a text through auditory and visual prompting.
Materials	Copies of selected text.
Time	20–30 minutes

Procedure

Step 1	Pass out enough copies of the text excerpt so that each student has one.
Step 2	Collaborate with the students to assign sounds and actions for each character in the selected text. Ask two or three students to choral read each character. (Choral reading involves more than one student reading the text simultaneously.)
Step 3	Read the text with the students in a large group and discuss the following: Were the sounds and actions appropriate for each assigned character? How do the characters look? What do you know about the characters that you didn't know before? How did the sounds and actions change your understanding of the text? What questions do you have about these characters?
IRA/NCTE Standards	1. Students read a wide range of print and non-print texts to build an understanding of texts, of themselves, and of the cultures of the United States and the world; to acquire new information; to respond to the needs and demands of society and the workplace, and for personal fulfillment. Among these texts are fiction and nonfiction, classic, and contemporary works. 2. Students read a wide range of literature from many periods in many genres to build an understanding of the many dimensions (e.g., philosophical, ethical, aesthetic) of human experience. 3. Students apply a wide range of strategies to comprehend, interpret, evaluate, and appreciate texts. They draw on their prior experience, their interactions with other readers and writers, their knowledge of word meaning and of other texts, their word identification strategies, and their understanding of textual features (e.g., sound-letter correspondence, sentence structure, context, graphics).

Exhibit 3.4 shows Katie's introductory lesson for Walt Whitman's *A Noiseless Patient Spider*. She used it every time she taught the American transcendentalists. Handouts for the lesson can be found in Exhibits 3.5 and 3.6.

Exhibit 3.3   Epic of Gilgamesh Character Assignments and Sample Script

Characters	Description	Make Sound-Say Phrase/Perform Action (performed by student actor)
Gilgamesh	A Sumerian king and ruthless ruler who abused his power and subjected his people to oppression.	*grunt* "HUUUUH!" *Flex muscles*
Enkidu	A man/beast created by Aruru - the Sumerian creator goddess (at the request of the populace of Uruk) to defeat Gilgamesh.	"Arooooo!!" *raise head and howl*
Anu	The "creator" god of the Sumerian pantheon, and father of the gods.	My "children" *smile proudly, moving move right arm/palm up, from left to right*
Enlil	The leader of the Sumerian pantheon (Anu relinquished his power to Enlil at some point), who was the instigator of the great flood.	"Whsssssssshhhh!" *move arms like you are swimming*
Shamash	The Sumerian sun god, who assists Gilgamesh and Enkidu in their battle with Humbaba because of a promise to Ninsun to protect Gilgamesh	"It's hot in here!" *wave hand to face to cool off*

Script (With Student Sound Effects Written in Bold)

Enlil (Whsssssssshhhh! *move arms like you are swimming*) of the mountain, the father of the gods, had decreed the destiny of Gilgamesh (*grunt* "HUUUUH!" *Flex muscles*). So Gilgamesh (*grunt* "HUUUUH!" *Flex muscles*) dreamed and Enkidu ("Arooooo!!" *raise head and howl*) said, The meaning of the dream is this. The father of the gods, Anu ("My children" - *smile proudly, moving move right arm/palm up, from left to right*) has given you kingship, such is your destiny, everlasting life is not your destiny. Because of this, do not be sad at heart, do not grieve or be oppressed. . . ..But do not abuse this power, deal justly with your servants in the palace, deal justly before Shamash (It's hot in here! *wave hand to face to cool off*).

Exhibit 3.4 Walt Whitman's "A Noiseless Patient Spider" Lesson Plan

During-Reading Lesson	Making Connections
Objective	To identify key vocabulary and themes in a shorter text, applying kinesthetic reading strategies to develop textual comprehension.
Materials	2 or 3 beach balls, string, and slips of paper with key vocabulary words
Time	30–40 minutes

Procedure

Step 1	Pass out the vocabulary words identified in the accompanying worksheet. Arrange the students in a circle in the classroom. (This can be done! Katie had 28–32 students in a circle in her classroom.) In the circle, the students will say a vocabulary word and then "gently" throw the ball to another classmate in the circle. Once the students have tossed the beach ball to classmates while saying their vocabulary word, add the other balls, one at a time. By the time the students have completed this part of the lesson, three beach balls are being tossed around the circle.
	After about five minutes of beach-ball tossing, the students will have heard all the vocabulary words numerous times. Ask the students the following question: "You've heard words from the poem that we are about to read. What do you think the poem might be about?"
	Allow the students to predict what they think the poem might be about and discuss.
Step 2	The students are still in the beach-ball circle. This time, explain to the students that they will say their word and instead of tossing a beach ball, we will exchange string. The teacher should start the string toss. So it works like this: The teacher says the vocabulary word while holding the string. The teacher holds the end of the string and then tosses the ball of string to a student. The student who catches the ball of string holds on to the end and then tosses the ball to another student. By the end of the activity, all the students will be holding the sting and will have created a giant web in the circle. This will take about 10 minutes to complete the giant string web.

Exhibit 3.4 *(continued)*

During-Reading Lesson	**Making Connections**
	Once every student holds the string, read the entire text of "A Noiseless Patient Spider" and have a large-group discussion. These questions can help to introduce the students to transcendental themes: 1. What happens if one of us lets go of the string? What happens when it's pulled or dropped? In Katie's classes they would often realize that they are all connected to the string web and an individual's actions can influence the entire web. 2. What do you think Whitman is trying to tell the reader in his poem? 3. How do your actions influence a larger group? 4. How can your actions affect a larger group? This portion of the lesson takes about 5–10 minutes.
Step 3	Ask the students to let go of their string at the count of three: 1-2-3 Drop. This always has a dramatic effect on the students. Give them copies of the poem so they can refer to it if they wish. Ask the students to respond to the following in writing (their responses can be written in journals): How do individuals affect larger groups and events? What have you learned from this activity and why is it important? The students can discuss in small groups after they write their responses or there can be a large-group discussion. This lesson segment takes about 15 minutes.
IRA/NCTE Standards	1. Students read a wide range of print and non-print texts to build an understanding of texts, of themselves, and of the cultures of the United States and the world; to acquire new information; to respond to the needs and demands of society and the workplace, and for personal fulfillment. Among these texts are fiction and nonfiction, classic, and contemporary works. 2. Students read a wide range of literature from many periods in many genres to build an understanding of the many dimensions (e.g., philosophical, ethical, aesthetic) of human experience. 3. Students apply a wide range of strategies to comprehend, interpret, evaluate, and appreciate texts. They draw on their prior experience, their interactions with other readers and writers, their knowledge of word meaning and of other texts, their word identification strategies, and their understanding of textual features (e.g., sound-letter correspondence, sentence structure, context, graphics).

Exhibit 3.5 "A Noiseless Patient Spider" Handout 1

Directions: Cut up these words and give one to each student in your class. You can have duplicate vocabulary words if necessary.

noiseless	ductile
promontory	venturing
isolated	anchor
filament	soul
gossamer	unreeling
ceaselessly	musing
tirelessly	spheres

Exhibit 3.6 "A Noiseless Patient Spider" Handout 2

Directions: Make copies to distribute to students.

A Noiseless Patient Spider by Walt Whitman

A noiseless, patient spider,

I mark'd, where, on a little promontory, it stood, isolated;

Mark'd how, to explore the vacant, vast surrounding,

It launch'd forth filament, filament, filament, out of itself;

And you, O my Soul, where you stand,

Surrounded, surrounded, in measureless oceans of space,

Ceaselessly musing, venturing, throwing, — seeking the spheres, to connect them;

Till the bridge you will need, be form'd — till the ductile anchor hold;

Till the gossamer thread you fling, catch somewhere, O my Soul.

Teaching the Classics in the Inclusive Classroom

Creating Graphic Novels

Many students readily admit that they learn better when they associate pictures with the words in a book. Figure 3.1 is a template to use to have students create their own graphic novels. Figure 3.2 shows an example of how a graphic novel can be used created by Brad's student Joanna Nika, and Exhibit 3.7 provides a lesson plan.

Brad used this strategy with his class when they were reading *The Scarlet Letter* by Nathaniel Hawthorne. The original text of *The Scarlet Letter* can be very difficult to read, but by using the graphic novel format, students who were initially turned off or were having trouble gaining a deeper understanding of the text were able to understand greater details of the story.

Providing students with the opportunity to draw and visualize the reading as they see fit helps students to further understand and process the story. By using this form of visual learning, students increase their understanding and metacognitive thinking.

Figure 3.1   Graphic Novel Template

Caption _____	Caption _____	Caption _____
Caption _____	Caption _____	Caption _____
Caption _____	Caption _____	Caption _____
Caption _____	Caption _____	Caption _____

Summary:

Teaching the Classics in the Inclusive Classroom

Figure 3.2   Graphic Novel Example

Scarlet Letter Graphic Novel

Label each cell as a separate chapter. Give each cell a caption and draw a picture representing each chapter.

Exhibit 3.7   Graphic Novel Lesson Plan

During-Reading Lesson	Graphic Novels
Objective	Students will identify key events and illustrate these key scenes. In this activity, the students will develop comprehension skills, particularly in sequencing, summarizing, and analyzing.
Materials	Colored pens, pencils, marker, and graphic novels template
Time	30–40 minutes

Procedure

Step 1	Arrange students into groups of three. Instruct the students to complete a graphic novel template. In brief the students will brainstorm the key events from a recently read text.
Step 2	Once the students identify the key events, they should select eight and follow the directions in Handout 2. The students will illustrate the selected key events.
Step 3	The students should share their storyboards with their classmates and explain why they chose their selected key events. Added detail in illustrated scenes can be rough indicators of comprehension. In general, more details in a picture can indicate a greater understanding and comprehension of a text. Carefully consider what scenes the students identify. Are they identifying scenes that shape and affect the plot of the text? Do the illustrations indicate a particular point of view?
IRA/NCTE Standards	1. Students read a wide range of print and non-print texts to build an understanding of texts, of themselves, and of the cultures of the United States and the world; to acquire new information; to respond to the needs and demands of society and the workplace; and for personal fulfillment. Among these texts are fiction and nonfiction, classic, and contemporary works. 2. Students read a wide range of literature from many periods in many genres to build an understanding of the many dimensions (e.g., philosophical, ethical, aesthetic) of human experience. 3. Students apply a wide range of strategies to comprehend, interpret, evaluate, and appreciate texts. They draw on their prior experience, their interactions with other readers and writers, their knowledge of word meaning and of other texts, their word identification strategies, and their understanding of textual features (e.g., sound-letter correspondence, sentence structure, context, graphics).

Reader's Theater

We have an innate interest in stories. Telling and listening to stories is simply a characteristic of being human. The origins of this practice can be traced all the way back to the paintings found on the caves of our prehistoric ancestors.

Reader's theater is minimal theater that builds on this foundation for storytelling. In short, reader's theater puts literature into a simple dramatic form that engages an audience. This minimal theater builds on literature and readings and supports students' developing reading skills in

- Imagining pictures as the text is read
- Improving reading fluency through multiple readings of the text and practice with a selected text
- Creating interest and skill in reading
- Practicing and improving skills in reading for meaning and inference

The fact that *reader* is in the term *reader's theater* suggests that the reader is the main focus of this activity. There are no props, costumes, or strategies. Reader's theater is presentational, not representational, and the images from the text are not created on the stage but rather in the minds of the readers.

It is also a helpful tool for struggling readers and students with special needs because it is another way in which to examine and experience text. Given the linguistic complexity of many of the classic literary texts that are a mainstay in our literature curricula, it is an effective strategy for supporting students as they attempt to decode and interpret text.

Following is an example of reader's theater from *King Arthur and the Knights of the Round Table:* the tale of Sir Gawain and the Green Knight, translated by Sir Thomas Mallory.

ARTHUR: Thou shalt promise me by the faith of thy body, when thou hast jousted with the knight at the fountain, whether it fall ye be on foot or on horseback, that right so ye shall come again unto me without making any more debate.

GRIFLET: I will promise you as you desire.

NARRATOR: Griflet took his horse in great haste, and dressed his shield and took a spear in his hand. He rode a great wallop till he came to the fountain and thereby he saw a rich pavilion and thereby under a cloth stood a fair horse well saddled and bridled, and on a tree a shield of diverse colors and a great spear.

Griflet smote on the shield with the butt of his spear, that the shield fell down to the ground.

With that, the fair knight came out of the pavilion.

GRIFLET: For I will joust with you.

KNIGHT: It is better ye do not, for ye are but young and late made knight and your might is nothing to mine.

GRIFLET: As for that, I will joust with you.

KNIGHT: That is me loath but sith I must needs, I will dress me thereto. Of whence be ye?

GRIFLET: Sir, I am of Arthur's court.

Tips

To begin creating reader's theater scripts, check these sources: novels, poems, short stories, and essays. You may also pull scripts from Web sites such as Screenplays for You (http://sfy.ru).

Select a text for the script. Choose a text that supports many different voices. Assign readers for the different parts and begin to edit.

Suggestions for editing the script for performance

- Omit superfluous characters.
- Decide who will be the narrator.
- Determine whether a reader can portray multiple roles.
- Create a focus for the script.
- Edit the text so that only the most essential information that develops the story is included.

Suggestions for practice and rehearsal

- All parts should be clearly marked.
- Assign numbers for readers.
- The script should flow.
- There should be a balance of voices among the readers.
- Confirm that the script, with the edits, still flows logically.

Suggestions for the script format

- Begin with a title page, with text title and author.
- Characters should be clearly designated in the script.
- Check that performance directions are clearly marked.

The following is an example of an evaluation form.

Example: Reader's Theater Evaluation

Text Selected_____

Author_____

Readers_____

Tone of the Introduction to the Reader's Theater Selection (5 points):

☐ The actors created the proper tone for the reader's theater selection.

☐ The audience became interested in the selected piece.

Development and Use of Script (5 points):

☐ Script is edited and developed so that the audience understands the plot and characters of the selected text.

Performance (5 points):

☐ The author's performances effectively employ voice and gestures to develop the different characters and plots of the reader's theater script.

☐ Pauses and utterances are appropriately placed.

☐ Readers clearly rehearsed and developed their performances.

A reader's theater lesson plan is shown in Exhibit 3.8. The rubric follows in Exhibit 3.9.

Exhibit 3.8   Reader's Theater Lesson Plan

During-Reading Lesson	Reader's Theater
Objective	To use role-playing and dramatic performance as a tool to develop a personal connection with canonical text, as well as an understanding of the themes and major plots of canonical text
Materials	None
Time	1–2 class periods

Procedure	
Step 1	Before the students read a text, take a basic theme from the canonical work or from a few of the chapters and instruct students to create a situation in which they reenact that same theme.
Step 2	Have the students enact the scenes for their classmates.
Step 3	Conduct a large-group discussion about the themes and ideas that were presented by the different student groups. Bridge the information that the students presented in their presentations to the text that they're about to read.
IRA/NCTE Standards	**3.** Students apply a wide range of strategies to comprehend, interpret, evaluate, and appreciate texts. They draw on their prior experience, their interactions with other readers and writers, their knowledge of word meaning and of other texts, their word identification strategies, and their understanding of textual features (e.g., sound-letter correspondence, sentence structure, context, graphics). **12.** Students use spoken, written, and visual language to accomplish their own purposes (e.g., for learning, enjoyment, persuasion, and the exchange of information).

Exhibit 3.9   Rubric for Reader's Theater Lesson

✓+	Exceeds standards	Student has demonstrated a strong understanding of the theme through the creative output of the role-play. The role-play is creative and demonstrates originality.
✓	Meets standards	The role-play demonstrates the student's understanding and interpretation of the theme or topic.
✓–	Does not meet standards	The role-play does not demonstrate the student's understanding or interpretation of the topic.

Teaching the Classics in the Inclusive Classroom

Character Bookmarks

"Keeping all of those characters straight is making me nuts!" cried Terrence a 12th grader in a large group discussion of *King Lear*.

Oral review in large group class discussion was insufficient for students to recognize and connect the characters in a given text. Both efficient and struggling readers often express difficulty in keeping the characters straight in a complex text like a Shakespeare play, a Homer epic, or an Austen novel. Of course, recognizing and internalizing the roles of the characters is an important element as the students work toward the comprehension of a given text. Although charts, diagrams, and class discussions do aid the students to retain all of the characters' roles and relationships in a given text, they still struggle. This is where the characet bookmark can be a handy tool for the students as they read through a text. As we used character bookmarks, we discovered that the accessibility as the students read and the visual images supported the students as they internalized the characters' roles.

Using character bookmarks allows students to maintain an understanding about the characters of a story by listing the names and traits of the characters on the bookmark they are using in the classroom.

Character bookmarks were a discovery that Katie made when she taught Dickens's *Great Expectations*. The students complained that it was difficult to keep the characters straight in the novel. This handy tool aids the students in understanding the roles of the characters.

Figure 3.3 is a template, and Figures 3.4 and Figure 3.5 offer some examples. Exhibit 3.10 shows the lesson plan for this tool.

Exhibit 3.10   Character Bookmarks

Materials: Copies of the Character Bookmark Template (Figure 3.3) and sample Character Bookmarks (Figures 3.4 and 3.4) markers, or color pencils.

Time: 15-20 minutes

Step 1: Instruct the students that there are many characters to monitor in the novel that we are reading in class. Each student should receive a character bookmark template. This simple tool will support the students' text comprehension and understanding of characterization.

Step 2: Model for the students how to document the different character on their bookmark templates. You can use the samples that are found in Figures 3.4 and 3.3.

Step 3: The students can review the different characters that they have already encountered in their reading and place them on their bookmark. It is helpful to use different colors for the characters.

Exhibit 3.10 (*continued*)

Step 4: Instruct the students that they will record new characters as they encounter them on their bookmark and also add more information about characters that they have already documented.

IRA/NCTE Standard

2. Students read a wide range of literature from many periods in many genres to build an understanding of the many dimensions (e.g., philosophical, ethical, aesthetic) of human experience.

3. Students apply a wide range of strategies to comprehend, interpret, evaluate, and appreciate texts. They draw on their prior experience, their interactions with other readers and writers, their knowledge of word meaning and of other texts, their word identification strategies, and their understanding of textual features. , sentence structure, context, graphics).

Figure 3.3 Character Bookmarks Template

Use a half sheet of 8.5 by 11 paper and fold in half. As the students read a text, they can document the different characters on their character bookmark. Encourage the students to create diagrams and pictures to help them identify the characters

Title: _____

Character Bookmark — SIDE ONE

_____

Character Name _____

Add details and pictures in this space provided

Character Name _____

Character Name _____

Title: _____

Character Bookmark — SIDE TWO

_____

Character Name _____

Character Name _____

Character Name _____

Figure 3.4 Character Bookmarks—*Romeo and Juliet*

Romeo and Juliet

Character Bookmarks – SIDE ONE

Capulets:

Juliet: Only daughters of family. Loves Romeo. Cousin of Tybalt.

Nurse: A comic character who took care of Juliet her whole life. She often provides comic relief when needed, and Lady Capulet depends on her for advice regarding her daughter.

Lord and Lady Capulet: Although they both truly love their daughter, neither one comes close to understanding Juliet's true feelings.

Paris: Lord Capulet arranges for him to marry Juliet.

Tybalt: Juliet's cousin who is tempestuous and teases Romeo. He is aggressive and violent.

Friar Lawrence: Friend to both Romeo and Juliet. He secretly marries the couples and is an expert in potions and plants.

Romeo and Juliet

Character Bookmarks – SIDE TWO

Montagues:

Romeo: Young son of the family

Loves Juliet

About 16 years old

Friends with Benvolio and Mercutio.

Lord and Lady Montague: Very minor characters but their presence is felt in the play. The Montagues and Capulets are lifelong enemies.

Friar Lawrence: Friend to both Romeo and Juliet. He secretly marries the couple and is an expert in potions and plants.

Benvolio: Romeo's friend and cousin. He tries to quiet conflicts in the play.

Mercutio: Romeo's friend. He loves wordplay and is a close kinsman of the Prince.

78

Figure 3.5   Character Bookmarks—*The Odyssey*

The Odyssey Character Bookmarks - SIDE ONE ITHACA Odysseus: Protagonist of the epic. Fought in the Trojan War and wants to go home to Ithaca. Husband of Queen Penelope and father of Prince Telemachus. He is known for being a strong, courageous, and cunning warrior. Athena protects him but Poseidon hates him. Telemachus: Odyesseus's son who was an infant when his father left to fight in the war. Penelope: Odyesseus's wife who waits for his return for 20 years. Penelope's Suitors: Antinous Eurymachus Amphinomus	*The Odyssey* Character Bookmarks - SIDE TWO THE VOYAGE HOME TO ITHACA Odysseus: Protagonist of the epic. Fought in the Trojan War and wants to go home to Ithaca. Husband of Queen Penelope and father of Prince Telemachus. He is known for being a strong, courageous, and cunning warrior. Athena protects him but Poseidon hates him. Athena: Goddess of wisdom and war. She protects Odysseus. Poseidon: Brother of Zeus; puts many obstacles in Odysseus's way when he tries to return home to Ithaca. Zeus: King of the gods who sometimes allows Athena to help Odysseus return home. Calypso: Falls in love with Odysseus when he lands on her island-home of Ogygia. Polyphemus: One of the Cyclopes (uncivilized one-eyed giants) whose island Odysseus comes to soon after leaving Troy. Polyphemus imprisons Odysseus and his crew and tries to eat them, but Odysseus blinds him. Circe: The beautiful witch-goddess who transforms Odysseus's crew into swine when he lands on her island.

Found Poetry

Discovering mood, theme, character, and imagery is the potential outcome of this activity called *found poetry*—a lesson that promotes close reading and interpretation of densely packed text.

Found poetry allows students to develop their own poetry. Students read the text as a class and find the images they like the best.

Separate the students into groups of five. Have each group write two sentences with imagery that they like on sentence strips and arrange strip on a board to make their own poem. This teaches students to appreciate creative writing and understand the concept of creative teaching.

Exhibits 3.11 and 3.12 each present a different found poetry lesson.

Exhibit 3.11 Found Poetry Lesson Plan 1: Kinesthetic

During-Reading Lesson	Found Poetry
Educational benefit	Active exploration and manipulation of text
Example	Hamlet's "To Be or Not to Be" speech from William Shakespeare's play, *Hamlet*
Materials	Strips of paper, each one with a line from a monologue in the play.
Time	15–20 minutes

Preparation	
Step 1	Identify the purpose for the during-reading activity: What information do you want the students to learn from the activity? What issues do you want to clarify in the activity? Character motivation? Character conflict? Theme? Choose a monologue that conveys the information that students need to learn.
Step 2	Write each line of this monologue on a separate strip of paper.

88

Exhibit 3.11 (continued)

During-Reading Lesson	Found Poetry
Procedure	
Step 1	Arrange the students in a circle.
Step 2	Hand each student a card with a line from the text, keeping the lines in sequence as you distribute the cards.
Step 3	As they sit in a circle, each student will act the line of the text.
Step 4	Have the group of students practice their lines of the monologues as a group a couple of times. These practice sessions can provide students with additional time to reflect on the text being read.
Step 5	The ultimate goal is to make it sound like one person is speaking.
IRA/NCTE Standards	**2.** Students read a wide range of literature from many periods in many genres to build an understanding of the many dimensions (e.g., philosophical, ethical, aesthetic) of human experience. **3.** Students apply a wide range of strategies to comprehend, interpret, evaluate, and appreciate texts. They draw on their prior experience, their interactions with other readers and writers, their knowledge of word meaning and of other texts, their word identification strategies, and their understanding of textual features (e.g., sound-letter correspondence, sentence structure, context, graphics).

Exhibit 3.12 Found Poetry Lesson Plan 2: Written

During-Reading Lesson	Found Poetry
Objective	Develops student skills in reading comprehension for linguistically rich text. Nurtures student ability to identify and apply knowledge of the following literary elements: mood, theme, character, and imagery.
Materials	Copies of selected text. For our example, we are using Edgar Allen Poe's short story "The Fall of the House of Usher" and sentence strips.
Time	20 minutes

Exhibit 3.12 *(continued)*

During-Reading Lesson	Found Poetry
Procedure	
Step 1	Text for this lesson can be selected in a variety of ways. For longer texts like novels, select a chapter or key section. For longer short stories like "The Fall of the House of Usher," choose specific pages; this may help the students better focus on the text.
Step 2	Place the students in cooperative-learning groups of three.
Step 3	In their cooperative groups, the students will examine the selected texts for images and brief passages (about eight words or less) and write them on a sentence strip.
Step 4	Ask the students to arrange their sentence strips into a poem that makes sense.
Step 5	Instruct the students to display their poems in the class and invite the students to read aloud.
Step 6	Have a large-group discussion with the students about the construction of their "found poem."
IRA/NCTE Standards	1. Students read a wide range of print and non-print texts to build an understanding of texts, of themselves, and of the cultures of the United States and the world; to acquire new information; to respond to the needs and demands of society and the workplace; and for personal fulfillment. Among these texts are fiction and nonfiction, classic, and contemporary works. 2. Students read a wide range of literature from many periods in many genres to build an understanding of the many dimensions (e.g., philosophical, ethical, aesthetic) of human experience. 3. Students apply a wide range of strategies to comprehend, interpret, evaluate, and appreciate texts. They draw on their prior experience, their interactions with other readers and writers, their knowledge of word meaning and of other texts, their word identification strategies, and their understanding of textual features (e.g., sound-letter correspondence, sentence structure, context, graphics).

This chapter addressed the needs of adolescent readers as they approach a linguistically complex text like those commonly found among the classics. It is in the "during reading" stage that readers begin to unlock the text and make inferences that personalize the text. This reflective process does not end when a reader completes a text. Rather, it is the beginning of this reflective process. In the next chapter we will examine after-reading activities and their usefulness in addressing larger thematic and global questions. Through this reflective process readers continue to discover personal and emotional connections with the text they read.

Chapter Four

After–Reading Activities

There was a time when after-reading strategies meant that literature students were assigned a three-part essay asking them to "explain why Macbeth is a tragic hero" or "argue and prove that Elizabeth Bennet in Austen's *Pride and Prejudice* was a woman before her time." If the after-reading activity was not a three-part essay, it was most likely a multiple-choice quiz in which students were required to answer questions that, arguably, determined what they *did not* know about a text rather than what they *did* know and understand about a text. The value of these kinds of activities is uncertain in developing a student's reflective understanding of a text. Those days, we hope, are drifting away like a scene in the rearview mirror as we drive away from that time and place.

The reading process, according to reader-response theory, unfolds in three stages: pre-reading, during reading, and after reading (Beers, 2000). As we have explained throughout this book, these three phases support students in their preparation for reading a given text. The activities that are in each of these phases guide students through their exploration of a given text and help them develop comprehension skills. The after-reading phase occurs when a student finishes reading a text. During the after-reading phase, readers think about what they knew before they read the text. Then they consider what they learned as they read the text and what personal connections may have been made. Finally, readers link this with their previous knowledge.

After-reading activities prompt students to think reflectively and read between the lines of the text. They carefully consider elements of the text to explore and consider deeper levels of meaning in the text. The after-reading activities prompt students to think about and understand a text.

After-reading activities are important because they

- Assist students in extending meaning
- Provide the opportunity for students to question what they don't understand in the text
- Connect the text to personal experience
- Provide opportunities to visualize the text
- Explore and summarize the text
- Identify key characters; main plot events; and other details, like symbols
- Develop inferences about the text
- Develop final conclusions about the text after careful reflection on what they have read
- Participate in larger discussions about the text and express their opinions about the text in a larger audience
- Identify the author's point of view and opinions

Exhibit 4.1 shows the after-reading strategies covered in this chapter along with the skill sets addressed by each strategy.

Exhibit 4.1   Strategies and Skill Sets

During-Reading Strategy	Appropriate for these Learning Styles	Multiple Intelligences
Character Biographies	Auditory	Visual/Spatial Logical/Mathematical Interpersonal
Character Questionnaire	Auditory Visual	Visual/Spatial Logical/Mathematical Verbal/Linguistic Intrapersonal
Character Book Bag	Visual Kinesthetic/Psychomotor	Visual/Spatial Logical/Mathematical Bodily/Kinesthetic Verbal/Linguistic Intrapersonal
Character Postcards	Visual Kinesthetic/Psychomotor	Visual/Spatial Verbal/Linguistic Intrapersonal
Mapping it Out	Visual Kinesthetic/Psychomotor	Visual/Spatial Logical/Mathematical Intrapersonal
Text Timeline	Visual Kinesthetic/Psychomotor	Visual/Spatial Logical/Mathematical Intrapersonal
Making Memories	Visual Kinesthetic/Psychomotor	Visual/Spatial Logical/Mathematical Intrapersonal
Movie Magic	Visual	Visual/Spatial Intrapersonal
Theme Sketches	Visual	Visual/Spatial Intrapersonal
I Saw It	Auditory Kinesthetic/Psychomotor	Bodily/Kinesthetic Interpersonal
Rapping Up the Text	Auditory Kinesthetic/Psychomotor	Musical/Rhythmic Logical/Mathematical Verbal/Linguistic

Character Biography

This lesson is an after-reading activity in which students can develop their skills in character analysis. The lesson plan in Exhibit 4.2 shows how to create a character biography.

Exhibit 4.2   Character Biography Lesson Plan

After-Reading Activity	Character Biography
Objective	To develop students' skills in character analysis and also develop students' writing process skills
Materials	Character questionnaire
Time	40–50 minutes

Procedure	
Step 1	In a large-group discussion, brainstorm with students the questions they might like to ask the characters in a text that they have just completed. Record the students' questions on an overhead transparency or poster paper. The character questionnaire included with this lesson was developed by students in Katie's high school classes.
Step 2	Assign students to pairs that will examine the same character. One student will play the interviewer and the other student will respond to the questions acting as the character from the selected text.
Step 3	The paired students will complete the questionnaire.
Step 4	Once the students have completed the character questionnaire, they can go into larger groups that examine the same character. The students can share their responses with their classmates and write a character biography story.

Exhibit 4.2 *(Continued)*

After-Reading Activity	Character Biography
IRA/NCTE Standards	**1.** Students read a wide range of print and non-print texts to build an understanding of texts, of themselves, and of the cultures of the United States and the world; to acquire new information; to respond to the needs and demands of society and the workplace; and for personal fulfillment. Among these texts are fiction and nonfiction, classic, and contemporary works.
	2. Students read a wide range of literature from many periods in many genres to build an understanding of the many dimensions (e.g., philosophical, ethical, aesthetic) of human experience.
	3. Students apply a wide range of strategies to comprehend, interpret, evaluate, and appreciate texts. They draw on their prior experience, their interactions with other readers and writers, their knowledge of word meaning and of other texts, their word identification strategies, and their understanding of textual features (e.g., sound-letter correspondence, sentence structure, context, graphics).

Character Questionnaire

The character questionnaire is an exercise that prompts the reader to examine characterization. The questions are detailed, prompting the reader to think creatively and precisely about the character's actions and role in a given text. Katie has found that the students enjoy the role playing since they have to get into the character's head and in some of the cases make assumptions to answer the questions posed.

Read the following questions. Choose the questions that you think will be most helpful in writing about your character. You can use these questions, as well as the ones from the class discussion.

What is your character's name?

Where is your character's birthplace?

What language does your character speak?

Does your character know other languages?

With what culture do most strongly identify?

How does your character express his or her cultural and historical identity?

Discuss a recent conflict and how your character handled the situation.

What does your character like to do during free time?

Who is your character's best friend?

Why is that person your character's best friend?

If your character could live anywhere in the world, where would he or she live? Why?

If your character could change anything in your life, what would that change be? Why?

Once the students have completed their character biography, they can use the following character questionnaire biography for self-evaluation.

Teaching the Classics in the Inclusive Classroom

Character Questionnaire

Self-Evaluation

Writer: _____

Writer's Comments:

- Evaluate your work objectively in a few sentences. What do you need to revise, change, or develop for the next draft?

- Discuss the problems you had with the draft, and explain where you think the problem areas are in your character biography.

- Make a list of the expectations you have for your revision partner or response group. How do you want them to assist you in your revision?

Character Book Bag

As with the character questionnaire and character biography, the opportunity to think like a specific character encourages readers to delve more deeply into the text. Activities like the character book bag in Exhibit 4.3 prompt them to think about the character and text in specific terms. Through this outside-inside process students can develop a personal connection with and understanding of a character and text. As we mentioned in previous chapters, this intimate, personal, and emotional interaction with texts boosts a student's engagement and comprehension.

Character Book Bag: Handout

Name _____

Name of selected character _____

Directions: Indicate each artifact that you selected and explain

    Why you selected the artifact

    How it represents your character

Artifact 1	Artifact 2
Artifact 3	Artifact 4
Artifact 5	

Exhibit 4.3 Character Book Bag Lesson Plan

After-Reading Activity	Character Book Bag
Objective	To make inferences about key characters through the text that was read and the selection of items to represent the character
Materials	Book bag and items that represent the character. The items for the book bag will differ for each student.
Time	20–30 minutes

Procedure

Step 1	The students should reflect on the characters from a recently read text. Prompt the students to picture the characters in their mind and what the characters might look like. The students should also be encouraged to consider what the character that they selected might carry around in a personal book bag. For example, in *Romeo and Juliet,* what would Juliet carry around in her book bag? Maybe she would carry a book of love poems or a personal journal.
Step 2	Instruct the students to select five items that they think would represent their selected character and place them in a bag to bring to class the next day. They should also complete the Handout that goes with this lesson.
Step 3	At the next class, the students can share their character book bags in small groups or with the entire class.
IRA/NCTE Standards	3. Students apply a wide range of strategies to comprehend, interpret, evaluate, and appreciate texts. They draw on their prior experience, their interactions with other readers and writers, their knowledge of word meaning and of other texts, their word identification strategies, and their understanding of textual features (e.g., sound-letter correspondence, sentence structure, context, graphics).
	11. Students participate as knowledgeable, reflective, creative, and critical members of a variety of literacy communities.

Character Postcards

As with previously discussed character exercises, the character postcard activity in Exhibit 4.4 is an opportunity for students to examine a character carefully and critically. Posing the question "What would this character write on a postcard?" prompts readers to reflectively consider the many elements that contribute to the character's actions. This is Katie's favorite activity to do with her students when they are examining character. The students always deliver clever and insightful glimpses of the characters.

Exhibit 4.4   Character Postcards Lesson Plan

After-Reading Activity	Character Postcards
Objectives	To interpret and represent a character through a postcard To visually represent a scene from the text
Materials	4-by-6-inch pieces of card stock and crayons, markers, or colored pencils
Time	20–30 minutes
Procedure	
Step 1	Create a two-column chart for the chalkboard or overhead projector with the following headings: Characters and Key Scenes.
Step 2	Brainstorm with the students the main characters from the text. Once the students have listed the main characters from the text, the students can either confer in pairs or small groups the key scenes for each of the listed characters.
Step 3	The key scenes should be listed with the characters for the chart on the chalkboard or overhead.
Step 4	Instruct the students to write a postcard from the character's point of view. On the other side of the postcard, the students should draw one of the key scenes from the text. The narrative should discuss and correspond to the postcard scene.

Exhibit 4.4 *(Continued)*

After-Reading Activity	Character Postcards
IRA/NCTE Standards	**3.** Students apply a wide range of strategies to comprehend, interpret, evaluate, and appreciate texts. They draw on their prior experience, their interactions with other readers and writers, their knowledge of word meaning and of other texts, their word identification strategies, and their understanding of textual features (e.g., sound-letter correspondence, sentence structure, context, graphics).
	11. Students participate as knowledgeable, reflective, creative, and critical members of a variety of literacy communities.

Mapping It Out

With complex texts like *The Odyssey* in which many events take place, it is often challenging for struggling readers to keep track of all the events. Katie found that oral review was not enough in many cases and decided to create activities like *mapping it out* that allow students to review key events from the text using the visual arts. Exhibit 4.5 outlines the steps in creating a plot map, and the sample in Figure 4.1 was created by a ninth-grade student who was mainstreamed into Katie's English class.

Exhibit 4.5 Mapping It Out Lesson Plan

After-Reading Lesson	Mapping It Out
Objectives	To review the plot and setting of a selected text To create a visual representation of the plot and setting
Materials	Plain paper, markers, crayons, and colored pencils
Time	30 minutes
Procedure	
Step 1	With the students, review the key plot events and settings of a selected text. This can be completed in a large classroom discussion or in small collaborative groups.
Step 2	Have the students take the key plot points and settings and create a map of the selected text. (See the sample from Homer's *The Odyssey* in Figure 4.1). The plot events should be in sequence and should reveal the students' understanding of the text.
Step 3	The students can discuss how they created their maps in small groups.
IRA/NCTE Standards	**3.** Students apply a wide range of strategies to comprehend, interpret, evaluate, and appreciate texts. They draw on their prior experience, their interactions with other readers and writers, their knowledge of word meaning and of other texts, their word identification strategies, and their understanding of textual features (e.g., sound-letter correspondence, sentence structure, context, graphics). **11.** Students participate as knowledgeable, reflective, creative, and critical members of a variety of literacy communities.

Teaching the Classics in the Inclusive Classroom

Figure 4.1 Sample Plot Map from *The Odyssey*

Text Timeline

When students find it difficult to keep track of all the events in a given text, the visual representation of key events often helps them process and comprehend it better. Exhibit 4.6 outlines the steps for creating a text timeline.

Exhibit 4.6   Text Timeline Lesson Plan

After-Reading Activity	Text Timeline
Objective	To sequence, interpret, and develop comprehension of key events in the classic being studied
Materials	Copies of the classic novel or play, long sheet of butcher paper, index cards, tape, crayons, markers, and colored pencils
Time	30–50 minutes

Procedure	
Step 1	Place the students into groups of three to five students.
Step 2	Ask the students to discuss and identify the key events in the classic being studied.
Step 3	Have the students list each event on a separate index card. As the students work on this activity in small groups, the teacher can post the butcher paper on a classroom wall. The teacher should draw a blank timeline on the butcher paper that resembles that of the classic being studied.
Step 4	Once the students have identified and written the key plot events on their index cards, focus their attention on the butcher-block timeline. Have the students organize their event index cards and use tape to place them on the timeline.
Step 5	Once the students place the event index cards on the timeline, remove any duplicates. Assign each group to illustrate one event from the timeline. (Katie likes to have all the students draw on the timeline together, but if it gets too crowded, the groups can do separate illustrations and tape or glue them to the timeline.)

Teaching the Classics in the Inclusive Classroom

Exhibit 4.6   (Continued)

Step 6	Once the students have completed the timeline and the illustration, ask them the following question (in discussion or as a journal prompt): What did they learn about the text from this activity?
IRA/NCTE Standards	**3.** Students apply a wide range of strategies to comprehend, interpret, evaluate, and appreciate texts. They draw on their prior experience, their interactions with other readers and writers, their knowledge of word meaning and of other texts, their word identification strategies, and their understanding of textual features (e.g., sound-letter correspondence, sentence structure, context, graphics).
	11. Students participate as knowledgeable, reflective, creative, and critical members of a variety of literacy communities.

Making Memories

Here's how to create a scrapbooking page about a text:

- Create a main idea or central theme for the page.
- Select two or three main colors for the page. Too many colors are distracting for the viewer.
- Pick one drawing, photo, or visual item to be the main focus for the page.
- Add text that explains the scene, character, or event.
- Add additional stickers, embellishments, and smaller pictures that develop your page theme.
- Arrange all of the items and then glue or tape them on the page.

A lesson plan for this activity appears in Exhibit 4.7, and Figure 4.2 shows a sample scrapbook page.

Figure 4.2   Sample Scrapbook Page

Grendel Emerges from His Cave

Grendel the demon, possessor of the moors, began his crimes.

He was of a race of monsters exiled from mankind by God.
He was of the race of Cain, that man punished for murdering his brother. From that family comes all evil beings—monsters, elves, zombies. Also the giants who fought with God and got repaid with the flood.

Teaching the Classics in the Inclusive Classroom

Exhibit 4.7 Making Memories Lesson Plan

After-Reading Activity	Making Memories
Objective	To reflect and extend comprehension of text
Materials	Paper, scissors, tape, folders, hole punch, fasteners, and markers
Time	5 class periods or an independent homework project

Procedure

Step 1	With the students, brainstorm the key characters and scenes that are pivotal to the text. Using large chart paper or butcher paper is helpful since the students' ideas can be posted while they are working on their scrapbooks.
Step 2	If possible, create a model scrapbook page and show the students what a scrapbook looks like. The following Web sites are helpful for the students to gain a sense of what the scrapbook phenomenon is about. http://www.scrapbookmemoriestv.com (Web site for the PBS series on scrapbooking) http://scrapbooking.about.com/library/weekly/aa053104a.htm (Simple steps for scrapbooking) http://www.homeandfamilynetwork.com/crafts/scrap.html (More basic tips for scrapbooking)
Step 3	Use the handout that lists the elements of a good scrapbook page.
Step 4	The students should select 5–10 scenes/events (depending on how long the teacher wants this project to be) and create a scrapbook page for each scene/event.
Step 5	The students can work independently or in class to create their scrapbooks. When the students have completed their scrapbooks, ask the students to add a page at the end, as their conclusion, that answers the following question: What did you learn about the book/text through your scrapbook that you didn't know before? Why is this important?
IRA/NCTE Standards	3. Students apply a wide range of strategies to comprehend, interpret, evaluate, and appreciate texts. They draw on their prior experience, their interactions with other readers and writers, their knowledge of word meaning and of other texts, their word identification strategies, and their understanding of textual features (e.g., sound-letter correspondence, sentence structure, context, graphics).
	11. Students participate as knowledgeable, reflective, creative, and critical members of a variety of literacy communities.

Movie Magic

The lesson plan in Exhibit 4.8 provides an additional opportunity for students to express what they know and understand about a text through the visual arts. The various pictures are interpretations of the same text. When students view different visual representations of a classic like *Macbeth*, they can begin to make connections about the various ways that people respond to and interpret texts. This approach can be a rich context in the classroom because the students often note that the visual representations reflect the time period in which they were created.

Following is a selection of Web sites where illustrations for this lesson can be found:

Library of Congress: www.loc.gov

Movie stills: www.movieweb.com

Academy of Motion Picture Arts and Sciences: http://www.oscars.org

Google Images: http://images.google.com (simply type in a character, text title, or author, and pictures from all over the Web will be searched; this is a fabulous research tool)

Tony Awards: www.tonyawards.com

Theater history: www.theatrehistory.com

Shakespeare's Globe Theater: www.shakespeares-globe.org

Exhibit 4.8   Movie Magic Lesson Plan

After-Reading Activity	Movie Magic
Objectives	To examine different interpretations of text
Materials	Various photos and stills from movies or illustrations of a selected text (see Web sites listed)
Time	One class period

Procedure

Step 1	Prior to class, select different visual images of a selected text. For this lesson, use Shakespeare's *Macbeth*.
Step 2	Place the students into groups of three or four students. Each group should have a variety of pictures that were created for *Macbeth*. In the groups, students should discuss the following: What feelings or mood is portrayed in this picture? What does the artist or director think about the different characters? Which pictures most closely represent how characters appear in the play?
Step 3	As a large group, discuss the different pictures and summarize the separate groups' findings.
IRA/NCTE Standards	**1.** Students read a wide range of print and non-print texts to build an understanding of texts, of themselves, and of the cultures of the United States and the world; to acquire new information; to respond to the needs and demands of society and the workplace; and for personal fulfillment. Among these texts are fiction and nonfiction, classic, and contemporary works. **3.** Students apply a wide range of strategies to comprehend, interpret, evaluate, and appreciate texts. They draw on their prior experience, their interactions with other readers and writers, their knowledge of word meaning and of other texts, their word identification strategies, and their understanding of textual features (e.g., sound-letter correspondence, sentence structure, context, graphics). **11.** Students participate as knowledgeable, reflective, creative, and critical members of a variety of literacy communities.

Theme Sketches

Visual representation of text, like dramatic representation, provides inviting pathways for struggling readers to examine and participate in the world of a given text. Theme sketches like those shown in Figure 4.3 require students to reflectively consider the scene from the text before they can create a visual representation. Reflection, interpretation, and comprehension are all necessary for students to successfully complete this activity (see the lesson plan in Exhibit 4.9).

Figure 4.3 Sample Theme Sketch

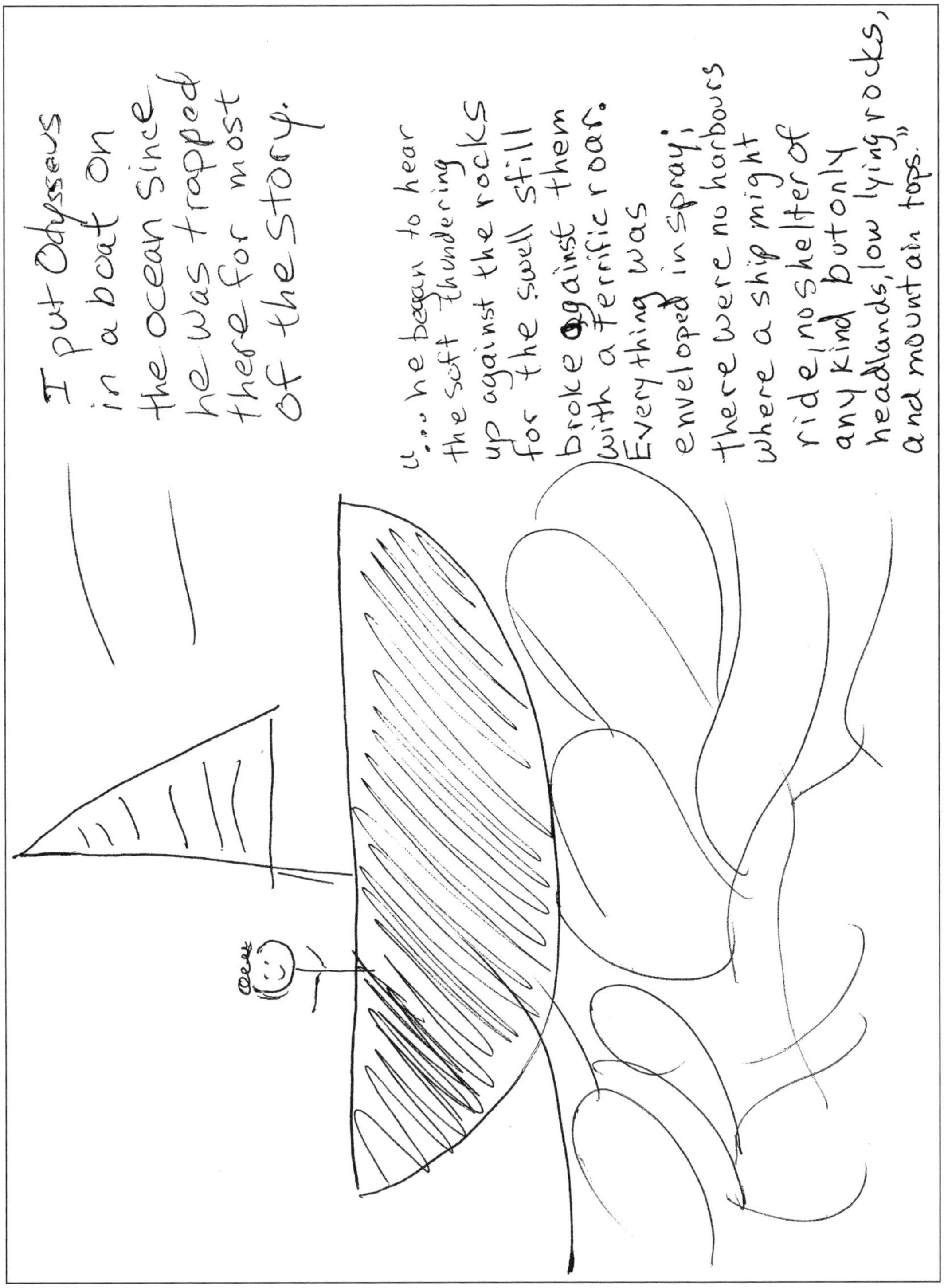
I put Odysseus in a boat on the ocean since he was trapped there for most of the story.
"... he began to hear the soft thundering up against the rocks for the swell still broke against them with a terrific roar. Everything was enveloped in spray; there were no harbours where a ship might ride, no shelter of any kind but only headlands, low lying rocks, and mountain tops."

Exhibit 4.9   Theme Sketches Lesson Plan

After-Reading Activity	Theme Sketches
Objective	To represent thematic understanding of text through visual representation
Materials	Plain paper, markers, crayons, and colored pencils
Time	A class period or independent work

Procedure	
Step 1	The students can work in pairs or independently for this lesson. The students are to create a sketch, or visual representation, of what they think the text means.
Step 2	Once the students have created their sketches, they should write 1–2 sentences explaining the idea behind their sketches.
Step 3	Once the students have completed their sketch, ask them to write on the back what they learned and why it is important.
Step 4	Put the students in small groups to share and discuss their sketches.
IRA/NCTE Standards	1. Students read a wide range of print and non-print texts to build an understanding of texts, of themselves, and of the cultures of the United States and the world; to acquire new information; to respond to the needs and demands of society and the workplace; and for personal fulfillment. Among these texts are fiction and nonfiction, classic, and contemporary works. 3. Students apply a wide range of strategies to comprehend, interpret, evaluate, and appreciate texts. They draw on their prior experience, their interactions with other readers and writers, their knowledge of word meaning and of other texts, their word identification strategies, and their understanding of textual features (e.g., sound-letter correspondence, sentence structure, context, graphics). 11. Students participate as knowledgeable, reflective, creative, and critical members of a variety of literacy communities.

Teaching the Classics in the Inclusive Classroom

I Saw It

Students often find it challenging to track all the key plot events in a complex text. The activity outlined in Exhibit 4.10 is designed to put the students in the text world as they dramatically retell the key events that drive the plot in a selected text.

Exhibit 4.10   I Saw It Lesson Plan

After-Reading Activity	I Saw It
Objectives	To recall and interpret key plot events from a text
Materials	A scarf
Time	About 20 minutes but depends on length of text

Procedure

Step 1	Use *Romeo and Juliet* as the text for the directions and explanation of the activity. Arrange the students in a circle and give the following directions while standing in the circle:
	"You are all citizens of Verona and were eyewitnesses to the events that involved Romeo and Juliet. It is our job to report the events as they happened to reporters and officials who arrived at the scene to investigate. Each of us will have the opportunity to explain what happened. One witness will speak at a time. When you have something to add to the retelling of the story, come to the center of the circle and take the scarf. Begin your retelling with "I saw" and add your detail. We will continue to hand off the scarf and take turns until all of us have had a turn. The only person who is talking is the one who is in the center of the circle with the scarf."
Step 2	As the teacher, model the beginning of the retelling. Hold the scarf and begin with a statement like, "I saw it happen in Verona. I was standing in the middle of the street when the Montagues and Capulets started to fight. They have been fighting with each other for as long as anyone can remember. They drew their swords in the middle of the marketplace and started to fight with each other." At this point, cue a student to jump in. The next student should take the scarf and continue the retelling. It might go like this, "I saw it too. They were fighting and all of a sudden the prince arrived to see the families fighting and he was furious. He was so angry that if he ever saw them fighting again the punishment would be death!"

(continued overleaf)

Exhibit 4.10 *(Continued)*

Procedure

Step 3	The teacher should continue to side coach but only when the retelling is slowing down or not accurate. The students should be encouraged to continue retelling the story and participating in the activity.
IRA/NCTE Standards	**3.** Students apply a wide range of strategies to comprehend, interpret, evaluate, and appreciate texts. They draw on their prior experience, their interactions with other readers and writers, their knowledge of word meaning and of other texts, their word identification strategies, and their understanding of textual features (e.g., sound-letter correspondence, sentence structure, context, graphics).
	11. Students participate as knowledgeable, reflective, creative, and critical members of a variety of literacy communities.

Rapping Up the Story

At the beginning of the year, when Brad taught his World Literature class, he had the students complete an interest inventory. He found that many of his students had an interest in hip-hop, or rap. As a result, when students were finished studying *The Epic of Gilgamesh*, Brad decided to have the students write, develop, and perform raps about the epic tale as a form of assessment of learning.

By summarizing canonical literature in a rap or poem, students can communicate their own understanding of the tale in musical performance art that they are comfortable with. Rap can be used as a form of auditory learning that challenges students to communicate the epic tales in their own words.

Exhibit 4.11 presents a lesson plan for Rapping Up the Story Project, and Exhibit 4.12 gives a rubric for the project.

The Epic of Gilgamesh Project

For this assignment, write a poem, song, or rap about *The Epic of Gilgamesh* or a scene from *The Epic of Gilgamesh*. Your song must have at least four verses and draw specific correlation to story. Your poem, song, or rap must be displayed on a poster.

The Epic of Gilgamesh Rap

written by Angel Delfi

Verse 1

Y'all can't mess with the Gilgamesh/
If you ain't productive enough you far from diligent//
Going toad to toad with this man you need some adrenaline/
With a side of pestilence, cause you can't mess with the kid//
Dude a one man army you better tuck in your skin/
Catch you like fish, he's gripping your fin/
And in the end, it's like France it's close to the fin/
You could ask Humbaba cause he ain't taking the win//
Couldn't go lucky if he all seven/
And he couldn't go 24 hours like 7/11//
Made the world feel threatening and the God's second/
But figure if he could conquer again the second time a blessing//
The half man, half amazing, to be half God is crazy/
People thought it's shady, to be killing on the daily//
Wishing everything was an improb like Wayne Brady/
Dude like Gilgamesh is less likely to be tired and lazy//

Verse 2

Let's postpone, Mesh and let's get to the flood/
Only way you surviving if you on a boat, or you a dove//
Cause everyone and they mama gone, so long/
This flood ain't ending till the fat lady finishes the song//
Gods shout out of wrath, whip out more than a half/

Death count? The Gods did their math//
Chances of surviving were like free throws from Shaq/
Gods' chances of underestimating was like Bush and Iraq//
Survival was unsuspected, then the Gods regret it/
Look back at their perspective, too late to be reflected//
The flood exculpated, it's too hectic/
Those who survive were consider mystic//
God's fatality, million casualties, choice of tragedy/
Even Gods had to face the reality//

Exhibit 4.11   Rapping Up the Story Lesson Plan

After-Reading Activity	Rapping Up the Story Lesson Plan
Objectives	To represent thematic understanding of text through auditory representation
Materials	Paper, pens, poster paper
Time	A class period or independent work
Procedure	
Step 1	The students can work in pairs or independently for this lesson. The students will create a rap or auditory representation of what they think the text means.
Step 2	Once the students have completed their rap, ask them to write it down on poster paper, then write on the back what they learned and why it is important.
Step 3	Put the students in groups of 4–5 students to share and discuss their raps. Students may perform their raps in front of the class.

Exhibit 4.11 *(continued)*

After-Reading Activity	Rapping Up the Story Lesson Plan
IRA/NCTE Standards	**3.** Students apply a wide range of strategies to comprehend, interpret, evaluate, and appreciate texts. They draw on their prior experience, their interactions with other readers and writers, their knowledge of word meaning and of other texts, their word identification strategies, and their understanding of textual features (e.g., sound-letter correspondence, sentence structure, context, graphics). **5.** Students adjust their use of spoken, written, and visual language (e.g., conventions, style, vocabulary) to communicate effectively with different audiences for a variety of purposes. **6.** Students apply knowledge of language structure, language conventions (e.g., spelling and punctuation), media techniques, figurative language, and genre to create, critique, and discuss print and non-print texts. **9.** Students develop an understanding of and respect for diversity in language use, patterns, and dialects across cultures, ethnic groups, geographic regions, and social roles.

Exhibit 4.12 Rapping Up the Story Rubric

16–20	Exceeds standards	This project: Demonstrates a strong understanding of the epic Contains a number of correlations to events and characters in the story Demonstrates a high level of creativity, research, and time invested on the project
10–15	Meets standards	This project: Demonstrates an understanding of the epic Contains correlations to events and characters in the story Demonstrates creativity, research, and time invested on the project
0–9	Does not meet standards	This project: Does *not* demonstrate an understanding of the epic Contains *few* correlations to events and characters in the story Does *not* demonstrate creativity, research, or an adequate amount of time invested on the project

After-Reading Projects

The following project ideas suggest ways students can demonstrate what they know and understand about a text. We often forget, as teachers of adolescents, that students can demonstrate what they know and understand about a text in a format other than a three-part essay.

- Create a model of a scene or important location from the text. Some examples include Boo Radley's house from *To Kill a Mockingbird* or the castle from *Macbeth*.
- Write a postcard to a friend, family member, the author, or to the character. Create artwork for one side of the postcard and write to your audience on the other side.
- Create a billboard or ad for the text.
- Write a song or create an instrumental piece that represents the theme of the text.
- Create a book cover. Include a description of the book that would interest potential readers.
- Go to an online bookseller's Web site and write a review and post it for other possible readers.
- Select a key quote from the text and paint or draw a picture that illustrates the meaning of the quote.
- Produce a file or video that reveals the students' comprehension of the text.
- Design a wall hanging for the classroom that reveals the theme and mood of the text.
- Write an opinion article about the characters and theme of the text.
- Present a mock trial about the play. Some suggested texts include *The Crucible* and *Of Mice and Men*.
- Make a travel poster for the setting of a text.
- Create a bumper sticker about the text's theme.
- Make a board game about the text.
- Design and make costumes for the characters.

The study of literature and story stems from our basic humanity; transcending time and culture, we share the need to tell and hear stories. Sharing stories should not be a frustrating experience for students. It should be an active and creative exploration. The activities in this chapter are designed to extend students' comprehension of the text and create opportunities to connect personally. This is key in motivating all adolescent readers.

In Chapters Two, Three, and Four, we examined how before-, during- and after-reading activities contribute to textual comprehension and engagement. As we prepared these chapters, we realized that the subject of writing was significant enough to warrant a chapter of its own. Chapter Five explains how writing in response to literature can be integrated before, during, and after the reading of a given text.

Writing Activities

Using writing strategies in the classroom can improve students' writing abilities, develop higher-order cognitive thinking, and increase their personal connection with literature; however, many teachers resort to using teacher-directed plot questions, as opposed to having students respond to literature. Here are some examples of teacher-directed plot questions for Shakespeare's *Romeo and Juliet:*

> Who can tell me why Juliet drank the sleeping potion?
>
> Why does Juliet's father threaten to throw her out of the house?
>
> Why does Friar Laurence help Romeo and Juliet?

Teacher-directed plot questions such as these were the means through which most of us read and studied Shakespeare's *Romeo and Juliet* when we were in high school. Even at fourteen, we understood that our English teacher expected only one answer—the one the teacher wanted to hear. Although teacher-directed plot questions such as these can support a reader's understanding of text, most students have ideas that go beyond the plot. Students wonder about Juliet's rebellion against her father and whether or not Juliet's love for Romeo was genuine. These issues were never explored in the class discussions or writing assignments when we were in high school. Our teachers rarely, if ever, invited us to explore the personal questions and issues that often drive young students to read. As high school students, we desperately wanted to discuss issues and ideas from this play that extended beyond teacher-directed plot questions.

Despite our highschool experience, we (Brad and Katie) both became English teachers and were determined to push our students beyond these plot-oriented questions. We both sought methods for teaching literature that evoked students' personal and emotional responses.

Reader-response theory asserts the possibility that there is more than a single response to a text and there are differences among readers and texts. In this time of test-driven curricula, writing in the classroom has taken a back seat to ensuring comprehension of the material. However, studies have shown that when students journal and write in class, their scores on standardized test-improve *more* than when writing is not an integral part of the literature curriculum. In addition, as teachers of literature (especially as teachers of the classics), we must remember that reading literature is not only an aesthetic and literary experience, it is also a personal experience. When students personally connect with literature, it provides a larger, more valuable, and empowering experience.

In this chapter, we describe writing activities that are successful in teaching the classics to students in high school classrooms. Many variables affect how students read and think about the classics, and these writing activities have been used with many different students with varied abilities in reading and writing. These strategies not only ensure that students comprehend the text, but they allow students to increase their personal interest in the text and develop methods for comprehending the material.

Exhibit 5.1 shows the learning styles and types of learners that are addressed by each writing activity covered in this chapter.

Exhibit 5.1   Strategies and Skill Sets

During-Reading Strategy	Appropriate for These Learning Styles	Multiple Intelligences
Journal Writing	Visual Kinesthetic/Psychomotor	Visual/Spatial Logical/Mathematical Bodily/Kinesthetic Interpersonal
Reader-Response Logs	Visual	Musical/Rhythmic Logical/Mathematical Verbal/Linguistic Intrapersonal
Creative Writing	Visual	Musical/Rhythmic Logical/Mathematical Verbal/Linguistic Intrapersonal
Freewriting	Visual	Musical/Rhythmic Logical/Mathematical Verbal/Linguistic Intrapersonal
Literature Letters	Visual	Visual/Spatial Intrapersonal
Character Diaries	Visual	Visual/Spatial Intrapersonal

Journal Writing

> A Fountain of Youth. A Fountain of Youth? How can a Fountain of Youth exist? Even if it did, why would I drink from it? I think I learn more from growing up than I would from that. I also don't think that I would change anything either. . . . I learn from my mistakes. At least I think that I do.
>
> Chastity's journal response to reading Hawthorne's short story, "Dr. Heidegger's Experiment"

Journal writing is an established practice for generating ideas for writing, and it is also a means for teaching literature (Fulwiler, 1987; Probst, 2004; Beach and Myers, 2001).

Academic journal writing—the process of writing personal thoughts or responses to a text in a notebook or journal—allows students to slowly develop a personal connection with their own writing and with the text they are reading. As the theory of reader-response states, the process of reading is an interaction between the reader, the text, and the context. Through journal writing, students can develop and create the context, or lens, for which they can view canonical literature.

Journal writing can do the following:

- Permit responses that are not constrained
- Allow students to tap into their personal knowledge
- Unlock the thematic ideas of the canonical text
- Provide students with the opportunity for reflection and contemplation of the text and their own thoughts and feelings
- Help students learn to write effectively
- Develop strategies to develop their higher-order thinking

The journal-writing activity can be used as a pre-reading, during-reading, or post-reading strategy. Journal writing offers the benefits shown in Exhibit 5.2.

Journal Prompts in Action

Charles, Katie's teacher and friend, uses journal-writing activities as motivators for the students. Before the students read a text, Charles's students usually participate in pre-reading activities. Charles often uses journal writing as a means of motivating the students with a text. For example, before the students read *To Kill a Mockingbird*, Charles thought of ways to tap into their personal knowledge. He asked whether they have ever visited the South or a rural place; then he asked that they put their answer in the form of a journal entry. Charles asked his students to describe it; if they haven't had this kind of experience, he asked them to imagine what it would be like. Charles shared his experience,

Teaching the Classics in the Inclusive Classroom

Exhibit 5.2   Academic Benefits of Journal Writing

Pre-reading	Allows students to access prior knowledge/experience and relate it to the text before reading
	Allows readers to nurture a preliminary connection to a text
	Can be used as a tool for students to break down and comprehend canonical literature
During reading	Can be used to assess comprehension of the text
	Can be used to increase comprehension of the text
	Helps develop a personal connection with the text, thus increasing comprehension
Post-reading	Helps develop a full understanding of the theme of the piece and its relation to readers' own personal lives
	Helps develop an understanding of the author's intent

As we discuss their journal responses, we talk about what the roads may be like. For example, what are the mosquitoes like at night? It really helps to create this image in the students' minds about what it is that we're going to start reading. They have this image of what it may be like to live in the setting of the book. They have a sense of what this time and place is really like. It's just that little something that helps them to relate to the reading.

This "little something," as Charles calls it, is important. Through the journal writing that students did in his class, students were invited to become involved in the text world of *To Kill a Mockingbird*. Thus they took the first step in becoming active participants in this text world.

Katie encouraged her students to explore themes, ideas, and characters prior to reading a particular text. When Katie taught Hawthorne's short story, "Dr. Heidegger's Experiment," she asked them to respond to the following prompt in their journals:

If you were standing in front of the Fountain of Youth, would you drink from it? If you could go back and change something in your life, what would you change? Why would you change it?

Over her time in the classroom, Katie feels she must have posed this pre-reading journal question to at least five hundred students. Their responses explored the thematic ideas presented in this short story prior to their reading. Their responses were as varied as students' lives normally are, but a few had more memorable lives than others. The example that follows demonstrate the thematic density of some literary texts, as students described their insights and explorations in their journals.

Oman—a shy, introverted student in Katie's sophomore English class—wrote:

> It would be interesting to drink from The Fountain of Youth and I think I would do it as long as I could switch back. I mean I'm not sure that I would want to stay fifteen forever. Like, what could I do? I mean I can't live on my own and I would be stuck in school forever. I might change some things but I wonder if I changed my things and what I've done if other people would notice. Would other people around be changed? I don't think people can change all that much.

Oman's response to the journal prompt reveals what often comes out about the four main characters in "Dr. Heidegger's Experiment": people are generally doomed to consistently repeat the same mistakes over and over.

Through their journal responses, Oman and Chastity demonstrate that they have unlocked the thematic ideas from Hawthorne's short story. This process of reflection that journal writing creates is that little something extra that Charles described and that encourages and invites the students to explore the text. To help students unlock these thematic ideas, teachers must take the step of creating and using challenging journal questions to which students can respond.

Creating and Implementing Journal Prompts in the Classroom

The students' responses were developed over time. These students did not respond so candidly when they first were asked to respond to journal prompts; their ability to express their thoughts and feelings on paper took time to develop. As is true of writing, constructing meaning and developing a personal response to literature is a process.

When they use journal responses for the first time in class, teachers will find that it takes time for students to accept that no single answer is expected from them and that their opinions and thoughts will be accepted. It may take as many as five to ten journal responses for students to start to be able to reflect on their personal response.

The purpose of the journals is to allow students to develop personal connections with the text, in order to increase their own comprehension of the intent of the author, as well as to question their own perception of the literature. Therefore, journal responses should be graded on effort or on completion of the task, *not* on grammar or the accuracy of the response.

When creating journal prompts, start by referring back to the section on creating questions in Chapter One.

Teaching the Classics in the Inclusive Classroom

Guidelines for Creating Effective Journal Prompts

When creating inquiry questions for canonical text, try to create prompts that

- Allow students to directly relate thematic events in the literature to events in their present-day lives
- Do not require a yes-or-no response and are thought provoking
- Tie in the themes of the canonical literature with personal reflection

Examples of Weak Journal Prompts

Weak question: In *The Scarlet Letter,* what did Hester Prynne do when she saw Arthur Dimsdale standing on the scaffold surrounded by the townspeople so early in the morning?

Weak because it only requires the student to pull the information directly from the text.

Improved question: In *The Scarlet Letter,* what did Hester Prynne do when she saw Arthur Dimsdale standing on the scaffold surrounded by the townspeople so early in the morning? If you were Hester, would you have responded the same way? Why or why not?

Better because it requires students to reflect on their own actions in that situation and to expand on their response.

Weak question: In *The Scarlet Letter,* do you think Hester Prynne was treated fairly?

Weak because students only have to answer with a yes-or-no answer

Improved question: In *The Scarlet Letter,* do you think Hester Prynne was treated fairly? How would her situation have been different if the story was written in the present?

The addition of the follow-up question allows students to develop a personal connection with the text and perspective on how things were different for people at a different time in history.

Follow-Up Discussion to Journal Entries

As shown in the examples, the use of journal prompts can lead directly to a class discussion about the responses. Again, it will take time for students to become comfortable sharing their responses, but this comfort level can be increased. To start, it may be helpful to ask if anyone feels comfortable sharing their responses. Focus on the students' opinions and repeat what they say, in order to elicit further reflection. For additional suggestions for eliciting class discussions, refer to Chapter One: Student Voice, Discussion, and Lecture.

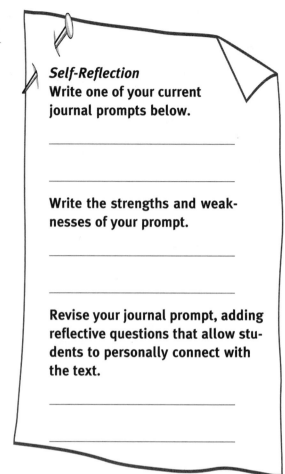

Self-Reflection
Write one of your current journal prompts below.

_____

_____

Write the strengths and weaknesses of your prompt.

_____

_____

Revise your journal prompt, adding reflective questions that allow students to personally connect with the text.

_____

_____

Reader-Response Logs

Reader-response logs provide students with a structure for taking notes while they read without limiting them to only one correct answer. They give students a chance to explore and reflect on their initial impressions and ideas about the text they are reading. Exhibit 5.3 offers suggestions for a reader-response log, and Exhibit 5.4 shows a sample activity that works well across grade levels.

Exhibit 5.3   Reader-Response Log Template

Name_____   Date_____

Entry 1

Setting (Time and Place)	**Event (Conflict, Touching Passage, Important Information, Something You Question)**	**Memorable Quote from Book (page number)**

Entry 2

Setting (Time and Place)	**Event (Conflict, Touching Passage, Important Information, Something You Question)**	**Memorable Quote from Book (page number)**

Creative Writing

Creative writing provides students with the opportunity to respond freely and create their own text world. Often creative writing is omitted from the English and language arts curriculum because it is deemed nonessential. We beg to differ. Through creative writing students gain the vital skills and ability to create text worlds as they experience and read classic literature. All writing, whether creative or academic, teaches kids how to express their ideas, which is an essential skill as our adolescent students mature into adult members of a democratic society. Creative writing provides students with the opportunity to respond freely and create their own text world. Often creative writing is omitted from the English and language arts curriculum because it is deemed nonessential. We beg to differ. Through creative writing students gain the vital skills and ability to create text worlds as they experience and read classic literature. All writing, whether creative or academic, teaches kids how to express their ideas, which is an essential skill as our adolescent students mature into adult members of a democratic society.

The following creative writing activity uses Marlowe's poem, "Come With Me and Be My Love" and Raleigh's response, "The Nymph's Reply to the Shepherd."

Exhibit 5.4   Creative Writing Lesson Plan

Creative Writing Activity	Come With Me and Be?
Objective	To provide the opportunity for students to respond to literature through a creative writing experience
Materials	Paper, writing utensils
Time	50 minutes
Procedure	
Step 1	Read and discuss the poems and explain how Raleigh's is a response to Marlowe's character. This takes about 20 minutes.
Step 2	Like Marlowe and Raleigh, the class will also write a paired poem. Divide the students into writing teams of three students. Each group will be assigned either "plea" or "response" in one of the following parings. The students will need to be divided into an even number of groups. The students generally take about 20 minutes to write their pleas and responses.

Exhibit 5.4 *(Continued)*

Creative Writing Activity	Come With Me and Be?
Step 3	Each group should read aloud their written piece. The students should read their pieces according to the pairings that are listed. The plea is read first and then the reply. See student samples that accompany this activity.
IRA/NCTE Standards	**2.** Students read a wide range of literature from many periods in many genres to build an understanding of the many dimensions (e.g., philosophical, ethical, aesthetic) of human experience. **3.** Students apply a wide range of strategies to comprehend, interpret, evaluate, and appreciate texts. They draw on their prior experience, their interactions with other readers and writers, their knowledge of word meaning and of other texts, their word identification strategies, and their understanding of textual features (e.g., sound-letter correspondence, sentence structure, context, graphics). **5.** Students employ a wide range of strategies as they write and use different writing process elements appropriately to communicate with different audiences for a variety of purposes. **6.** Students apply knowledge of language structure, language conventions (e.g., spelling and punctuation), media techniques, figurative language, and genre to create, critique, and discuss print and non-print texts. **11.** Students participate as knowledgeable, reflective, creative, and critical members of a variety of literacy communities. **12.** Students use spoken, written, and visual language to accomplish their own purposes (e.g., for learning, enjoyment, persuasion, and the exchange of information).

Some additional tips for "Come With Me and Be My Love" creative writing lessons.

Group Pairings for "Come with Me and Be My Love"?

Directions: Assign each writing team of three students either a plea or a response. The idea here is to mimic how poets like Marlowe and Raleigh responded to each other's work. Exhibit 5.5 suggests some possible plea and response pairings for the students.

Casting characters

Casting characters is an after-reading activity that prompts readers to delve into the details of characterization. By assuming the role of famous movie producers, the students are encouraged to cast an imaginary production of a recently read text. Exhibit 5.6 uses Arthur Miller's *The Crucible* as an example.

Exhibit 5.5 Creative Writing Activity: Plea and Response

Plea	Response
The student's plea for an A in the class	The teacher's response to the student
The blind date's plea to the prom queen	The prom queen's response to the blind date
The speeder's plea to the police officer	The police officer's response to the speeder

Another strategy for the exploration of character is the character résumé. As an after-reading activity, the students can select a major character from a given text and create a résumé. Through this activity the students delve deeply into a character's attributes, skills, and talents and discover more about characterization. Figures 5.1 and 5.2 are templates that can be used in the classroom for the character résumé activity.

Exhibit 5.6 Casting Characters

Creative Writing Activity	Casting Characters
Objective	To promote visualization of characters and development of student expression in writing
Materials	Paper, writing utensils
Time	20 minutes

Procedure

Step 1	Brainstorm and list the key major and minor characters of a recently completed text.
Step 2	Direct the students, working independently or in pairs, to assign parts to each character role. For example: *Congratulations! You have been hired by a major motion picture studio to direct* [insert text title] Take 3–5 minutes to assign roles. *Note:* One variation is to cut out pictures of actors from magazines or have the students draw the actors.
Step 3	The students can share their casting through one of the following groupings: Large-group discussion Think-pair-share Small-group discussion
Step 4	Let the students revise their casting if they so desire.
Step 5	Provide the students with the following voicemail message from their secretary: *The head of the studio has called, and he wants the casting and an explanation of the casting decisions. He wants this information in 10 minutes.*
Step 6	Break into the same sharing groups as in step 3 and have the students share their casting materials. See the example below of a possible cast call: *The Crucible* by Arthur Miller Cast Tituba: Whoopi Goldberg John Proctor: Robert DeNiro Elizabeth Proctor: Meryl Streep

Exhibit 5.6   *(continued)*

Creative Writing Activity	Casting Characters
	Rev. Parris: Keanu Reeves Rev. Hale: Brian Denehy Abigail Williams: Shannon Doherty Betty Parris: Hillary Duff
Step 7	Students should complete their casting by writing a note to the producer as the example demonstrates below: *Dear Mr. Big-Time Producer:* *I want to thank you for the opportunity to direct this production of Arthur Miller's* The Crucible. *Attached is my list of roles and the actors that I have assigned. I think that these actors can portray the personalities of these characters because I thought this is what they looked like as I studied the play. I think each of the actors will be able to convince the audience of this movie that they are actually the character.* *Sincerely,* *Director Dana*
IRA/NCTE Standards	**2.** Students read a wide range of literature from many periods in many genres to build an understanding of the many dimensions (e.g., philosophical, ethical, aesthetic) of human experience. **3.** Students apply a wide range of strategies to comprehend, interpret, evaluate, and appreciate texts. They draw on their prior experience, their interactions with other readers and writers, their knowledge of word meaning and of other texts, their word identification strategies, and their understanding of textual features (e.g., sound-letter correspondence, sentence structure, context, graphics). **5.** Students employ a wide range of strategies as they write and use different writing process elements appropriately to communicate with different audiences for a variety of purposes. **6.** Students apply knowledge of language structure, language conventions (e.g., spelling and punctuation), media techniques, figurative language, and genre to create, critique, and discuss print and nonprint texts. **11.** Students participate as knowledgeable, reflective, creative, and critical members of a variety of literacy communities. **12.** Students use spoken, written, and visual language to accomplish their own purposes (e.g., for learning, enjoyment, persuasion, and the exchange of information).

Figure 5.1   Mock Character Résumé

Macbeth

OBJECTIVE

To conquer any opponents to become King of Scotland

EXPERIENCE

Thane of Glamis
Thane of Cawdor

ACCOMPLISHMENTS

Vanquished traitors of King Duncan and displayed great valor in combat.

EDUCATION

Military education and received supernatural counsel from the three witches.

SKILLS

Can unseam enemies from the knave to the chaps.
Outstanding sword skills and military expertise.

Exhibit 5.7   Character Résumé Lesson Plan

Creative Writing Activity	Character Resume
Objective	Create a résumé for a character from a recently read text
Materials	Plain paper
Time	20 minutes

Procedure	
Step 1	Brainstorm and identify the main characters of a recently read text with the students.
Step 2	Provide the students with the résumé template (see Figure 5.3) and model with the class résumé writing. In the past, I have created résumés for Cinderella, Snoopy, and other commonly known characters with the students.
Step 3	Instruct the students to write a character résumé using the template provided.
IRA/NCTE Standards	**2.** Students read a wide range of literature from many periods in many genres to build an understanding of the many dimensions (e.g., philosophical, ethical, aesthetic) of human experience. **3.** Students apply a wide range of strategies to comprehend, interpret, evaluate, and appreciate texts. They draw on their prior experience, their interactions with other readers and writers, their knowledge of word meaning and of other texts, their word identification strategies, and their understanding of textual features (e.g., sound-letter correspondence, sentence structure, context, graphics). **5.** Students employ a wide range of strategies as they write and use different writing process elements appropriately to communicate with different audiences for a variety of purposes. **6.** Students apply knowledge of language structure, language conventions (e.g., spelling and punctuation), media techniques, figurative language, and genre to create, critique, and discuss print and non-print texts. **11.** Students participate as knowledgeable, reflective, creative, and critical members of a variety of literacy communities. **12.** Students use spoken, written, and visual language to accomplish their own purposes (e.g., for learning, enjoyment, persuasion, and the exchange of information).

Figure 5.2   Character Résumé Template

Character Name

Address of Character

Contact Info of Character

OBJECTIVE: [List the objective of the character.]

EXPERIENCE: [List any experience the character may have to accomplish his or her objective.]

ACCOMPLISHMENTS: [List any special accomplishments or awards this character has received.]

EDUCATION: [What is the character's education?]

SKILLS: [List any special skills this character has.]

Exhibit 5.8   Character Portraits: Picture Perfect

Creative Writing Activity	**Character Portraits: Picture Perfect**
Objective	To promote visualization of the text and develop artistic and creative responses to text
Materials	Plain paper, markers, crayons, colored pencils
Time	20 minutes

Procedure

Step 1	Brainstorm the major characters of a recently read text with the students.
Step 2	In paired student groupings, instruct the students to find passages that offer clues and/or direct description of a pre-selected character from step 1.
Step 3	Use the accompanying template (Figure 5.3) and direct the students, working in pairs or individually, to draw a picture of their character and complete the information that is requested on the template.
IRA/NCTE Standards	2. Students read a wide range of literature from many periods in many genres to build an understanding of the many dimensions (e.g., philosophical, ethical, aesthetic) of human experience. 3. Students apply a wide range of strategies to comprehend, interpret, evaluate, and appreciate texts. They draw on their prior experience, their interactions with other readers and writers, their knowledge of word meaning and of other texts, their word identification strategies, and their understanding of textual features (e.g., sound-letter correspondence, sentence structure, context, graphics). 5. Students employ a wide range of strategies as they write and use different writing process elements appropriately to communicate with different audiences for a variety of purposes. 6. Students apply knowledge of language structure, language conventions (e.g., spelling and punctuation), media techniques, figurative language, and genre to create, critique, and discuss print and non-print texts. 11. Students participate as knowledgeable, reflective, creative, and critical members of a variety of literacy communities. 12. Students use spoken, written, and visual language to accomplish their own purposes (e.g., for learning, enjoyment, persuasion, and the exchange of information.

Figure 5.3   Character Portraits: Picture Perfect Template

Figure:
Portrait of _____[character's name]_____

Quotes from the text that illustrate the character:

_____

_____

_____

My character is like _____

_____

_____

Description of character written by _____[student name]_____

Freewriting

Freewriting is similar to journaling and to keeping reading logs. What differentiates freewriting is that it allows students to express their thinking in a purely spontaneous manner. The spontaneity of this kind of writing prompts students to run the text through their conscience like a movie or slide show. Here are some suggested guidelines for freewriting:

- Ask students to write about the text continuously for five to ten minutes.
- Ask novice freewriters to briefly summarize what they've read and to comment about their reading; this helps them get into the mind-set of being a critical and active reader.

When the students complete their freewriting, encourage them to share with their classmates.

Students can also choose a word or phrase and write more about it. Peter Elbow (2002) calls this "looping." Students will have the opportunity to review and evaluate their own freewriting.

Freewriting should *never, ever* be evaluated or formally judged. Students need to know that they are not being graded, as this can lead to a loss of spontaneity. Instead of writing for themselves, students will write for their peers. Exhibit 5.9 outlines teaching strategies for freewriting in the classroom.

Exhibit 5.9   Freewriting Lesson Plan

Creative Writing Activity	**Freewriting**
Objective	To promote creative thinking, problem solving, and higher-order thinking
Materials	Plain paper and pen
Time	20 minutes
Procedure	
Step 1	Ask the students to spend 5 minutes writing freely, writing *whatever* comes to their mind.
Step 2	Model the writing process by showing a previous writing on an overheard or reading aloud a previous freewriting.
Step 3	Direct the students, working in pairs or individually, to draw a picture of their character and complete the information that is requested on the template.
IRA/NCTE Standards	**2.** Students read a wide range of literature from many periods in many genres to build an understanding of the many dimensions (e.g., philosophical, ethical, aesthetic) of human experience. **3.** Students apply a wide range of strategies to comprehend, interpret, evaluate, and appreciate texts. They draw on their prior experience, their interactions with other readers and writers, their knowledge of word meaning and of other texts, their word identification strategies, and their understanding of textual features (e.g., sound-letter correspondence, sentence structure, context, graphics). **5.** Students employ a wide range of strategies as they write and use different writing process elements appropriately to communicate with different audiences for a variety of purposes. **6.** Students apply knowledge of language structure, language conventions (e.g., spelling and punctuation), media techniques, figurative language, and genre to create, critique, and discuss print and non-print texts. **11.** Students participate as knowledgeable, reflective, creative, and critical members of a variety of literacy communities. **12.** Students use spoken, written, and visual language to accomplish their own purposes (e.g., for learning, enjoyment, persuasion, and the exchange of information).

Literature Letters

Literature letters are personal expressions that readers create in letter form about novels and stories. The letters are addressed to peers, teachers, or other interested parties, who may or may not have read the literature in question. When the study of literature is extended beyond the classroom community, the students are exposed to a larger literary community.

Literature letters allow students to convey their personal responses to literature and share them with other readers who are not in their immediate classroom community and teaches letter writing skills.

Here is an example of this extended reading community from one of Katie's tenth-grade students. The letter focuses on Hester Prynne from *The Scarlet Letter*.

Dear Mom:

I have not finished the whole book yet, but I have read enough to know that Hester doesn't like herself that much. She has to wear that scarlet letter on her dress and everyone in her town thinks that she is a bad person because she committed adultery. I think that everyone in the town should wear a scarlet letter because they have sins too. The only difference is that Hester got caught. Are sins only sins when people get caught?

Your Daughter,
Tanisha

Following is the excerpted response that Tanisha received from her mother.

Dear Tanisha:

I think that a sin is a sin if you know that you did something wrong. Just because other people don't know about it doesn't mean that it's not a sin. Do you think that people can overcome the sins that they committed? I think they can. It was a long time ago that I read A Scarlet Letter but I did remember how much I admired Hester's courage in the book. Keep reading and let me know what you think.

Love,
Mom

Students' literature letters often show that the letters are personal extensions of self. Literature letters do carry the possibility of expanding students' responses to a literary text. Once the boundaries of constructed, written response are lifted, students can develop a personal relationship with a text. If readers are given the opportunity to freely respond and are encouraged to engage a text, they can become more vested in the literature they read.

To begin using literature letters, have students respond to a journal prompt that asks them what they like and dislike about the book and why. In a

Figure 5.4 Literature Letter Template

Street Address
City, State, ZIP Code
Date

Dear _____,

Introduction (Explain why you are writing this person and what you will be telling him or her.)

Body of paper (Share with the person you are writing your experience reading the book: what you enjoy or dislike; be specific, referencing specific quotes from the book, if possible.)

Closing (Share what you would like from the person you are writing: whether you think they should read the book, ask whether they have read it before, and soon.)

Much Love (Sincerely, Thanks for Reading, or something similar)

(Sign your name here) _____

(Print your name here)_____

follow-up discussion, have them think about who they want to write to. Once this is done, use the template in Figure 5.4 to continue the conversation.

After the literature letters are written, make an additional assignment that requires that they receive a response back from a friend or relative.

After these assignments are completed, hold a class discussion or have students journal about what they learned from the experience. See Exhibit 5.10 for a lesson plan.

Exhibit 5.10 Literature Letters Lesson Plan

Responding to Literature Through Writing	**Literature Letters**
Objective	To promote and articulate personal response to literature through writing personal letters and to learn formal letter writing skills
Materials	Paper, writing utensils Personal stationery or colored paper
Time	This writing activity generally takes 20–30 minutes. Writing literature letters can take as long as one to two class periods, depending on the extent of the responses and the students' skills.

Procedure

Step 1	Review the format for letter writing (see the Literature Letter Template). Use the student samples that are included with this lesson.
Step 2	Instruct the students to write a letter to a parent or a friend about what they have just read.
Step 3	Place the students in pairs and instruct them to read aloud their drafted letter to their partner.
Step 4	Instruct the students to deliver their letters to the person addressed (parent or friend that is not a classmate). Request a response to the letter and return it to class. The responses can be shared in class.
IRA/NCTE Standards	**2.** Students read a wide range of literature from many periods in many genres to build an understanding of the many dimensions (e.g., philosophical, ethical, aesthetic) of human experience. **3.** Students apply a wide range of strategies to comprehend, interpret, evaluate, and appreciate texts. They draw on their prior experience, their interactions with other readers and writers, their knowledge of word meaning and of other texts, their word identification strategies, and their understanding of textual features (e.g., sound-letter correspondence, sentence structure, context, graphics). **5.** Students employ a wide range of strategies as they write and use different writing process elements appropriately to communicate with different audiences for a variety of purposes. **6.** Students apply knowledge of language structure, language conventions (e.g., spelling and punctuation), media techniques, figurative language, and genre to create, critique, and discuss print and non-print texts. **11.** Students participate as knowledgeable, reflective, creative, and critical members of a variety of literacy communities. **12.** Students use spoken, written, and visual language to accomplish their own purposes (e.g., for learning, enjoyment, persuasion, and the exchange of information).

Teaching the Classics in the Inclusive Classroom

Character Diaries

If students are to succeed academically, we must engage them academically. Brad had this in mind when he was teaching *The Epic of Gilgamesh* and used responses to a journal prompt to assess his students' involvement and engagement with the text. When the students walked in the room, he asked them to respond to the following question:

> How are you enjoying reading *The Epic of Gilgamesh* so far? What is your favorite or least favorite part of the epic?
>
> One student replied, "I don't get the story . . . it's really confusing."

Upon reflection, Brad realized that he needed to find a way to further engage the students. As a result, he decided to have the students write character diaries.

A character diary is a journal entry taken specifically from the point of view of one of the characters in the story. When writing a character diary, students' diary entries should reflect the unique qualities of the character, including rank or social position, sex, temperament, and personality. Character diaries allow students to express their understanding of the text in their own words through the point of view of one character. Here is an example from a student's journal:

Example: Gilgamesh's Diary

Day One of Quest

My city, Uruk, my people . . . oh, they love me so . . . why shouldn't they? I am wise, look fantastic, and know so much. What I don't get is why Aruru sent down this character, Enkidu. I mean, seriously, he's a beast!

Even though he is, I pinned him in four minutes . . . no one can beat me!

See the rubric in Exhibit 5.11 for a tool to evaluate character diaries.

Following is an example of a character diary assignment for Shakespeare's *Romeo and Juliet*.

Exhibit 5.11   Rubric for Character Diary Lesson

✓+	Exceeds standards	Student: Creates more than five diary entries Has more than one direct quote per entry Demonstrates an attempt to write in the style of the author/characters Demonstrates an understanding of the play/story Communicates the personality, temperament, sex, and social status of the character
✓	Meets standards	Student: Creates at least five diary entries Has at least one direct quote from the text per entry Demonstrates an understanding of the play/story Communicates the personality, temperament, sex, and social status of the character
✓–	Does not meet standards	Student: Has not created at least five diary entries Does not have at least one direct quote from the text per entry Has not demonstrated an understanding of the play/story Has not communicated the personality, temperament, sex, and social status of the character

Example: *Romeo and Juliet* Character Diaries

For this major assignment (100 points), you will assume the persona of a character in Romeo and Juliet and create an appropriate diary. The diary entry will reflect the character's unique traits: sex, rank, and social position, as well as personality and temperament. Remember, you are climbing inside this character's skin; you *are* this character. How does the character think? Feel? Believe? Why does the character do what he or she does? This activity stretches over the entire study of the play. I will give you time during classes to work on it.

Your diary will contain a minimum of five entries. Entries should show how the character grows and changes, based on what that character knows at certain points in the play. Include as much information from Shakespeare's text as possible in your journal entries. Quote the text directly at least once in each

Teaching the Classics in the Inclusive Classroom

entry. In fact, beginning with a quote may be a good jumping-off point for a creative exploration of the scene you plan to discuss in your entry.

Be creative. Tackle Shakespearean-sounding English or poetry for extra points (but only if you tackle it correctly and make sense!). If your character dies or disappears during the play, you must create a letter from another character who has "found" the diary and written an explanation of what happened to the character (and if Shakespeare didn't say, that means you get to be creative).

Divide into small groups with other writers. Edit each other's work. Revise your entries. Your final drafts must be free of errors and presented in a creative format (think back to the Oliver Twist newspapers, which many of you did so creatively. How can you make a character diary look as nice?)

Writing as response to reading literature is a powerful tool. Through writing students are encouraged to consider the texts that they read in a reflective stance. New discoveries about character, plot, and theme can be made through writing activities. Vocabulary is also taught through all stages of the reading process: before, during, and after reading. Chapter Six presents teaching activities that address vocabulary issues when teaching the classics in an inclusive classroom. In this setting it is even more critical to appeal to different learning styles and provide creative and eclectic teaching and learning activities.

Vocabulary Activities

Like most readers of this book, we frequently give our students long lists of vocabulary words and instruct them to write the definition of each one and use it in a sentence. After all, that's how most of us were taught vocabulary when we were students. Once we had memorized these words, we were given on a quiz, usually on a Friday. Today we know that this is not the most effective way to teach vocabulary. The charge today is to make vocabulary lessons *contextual*. But what does contextual mean in the classroom and how can we teach vocabulary to students with special needs? Another question is, How can we help students understand new words when they run across them in their reading. How can we help students use these new words them in their writing?

The task may seem overwhelming, but we can find answers to these questions. It's important to realize that ownership of vocabulary words does not come from memorization but from language experimentation and exploration. In short, we need to teach our students how to be language *detectives*. We can do that by considering the following as we teach:

Students need to study words, not memorize them.

Students need context clues. We can introduce strategies that allow students to use the text to discover the possible meaning of words.

We can teach students about the influences of other languages on English.

We can teach specific suffixes and prefixes to assist in understanding on familiar words.

We can instill the motivation to explore language and to find useful words.

In addition, it is imperative for all students that language study be active. It is especially important for students with special needs, as this can be an area of immense frustration for students. Therefore, in this chapter we offer lessons that employ more than one learning style, or intelligence, as well as provide students with opportunities to direct their own language study.

Tips

To begin creating vocabulary lessons suitable for preparing to read literature:

- Study word history and origins. (This is especially useful for British and world literature classes.)
- Study words and language patterns.
- Provide lessons that develop students' skills in using context clues to understand words.

- Use word chunks (such as prefixes, suffixes, or root words that build meaning for a larger word) to teach students about the building blocks of words.
- Develop lessons in which learning language is a game. Students need to learn how to manipulate language.
- Use graphic organizers and other visualization tools to help students learn about language and vocabulary.

Exhibit 6.1 shows the vocabulary strategies covered in this chapter and the skill sets addressed by each strategy.

The first year that Katie taught British literature to juniors, she was required to teach about the origins of the English language. In her eleventh-grade class, more than half of the students' first language was not English. As they explored the Angle, Saxons, and Normans in their quest to dominate that island, which was barely separated from the European continent, she discovered that her students liked to study about language. This interest was not unique to this class; it was true of most of her classes. When she queried her students, their responses indicated that they liked to know how words became part of everyday English. In other words, they became detectives in a mystery.

Teaching the Classics in the Inclusive Classroom

Exhibit 6.1 Strategies and Skill Sets

During-Reading Strategy	Appropriate for These Learning Styles	Multiple Intelligences
Anglo-Saxon Vocabulary	Visual Auditory	Visual/Spatial Logical/Mathematical Verbal/Linguistic Intrapersonal
Invading Words	Visual Auditory	Visual/Spatial Logical/Mathematical Verbal/Linguistic Intrapersonal
Norman-French Vocabulary	Visual Auditory	Visual/Spatial Logical/Mathematical Verbal/Linguistic Intrapersonal
Words in Action	Tactile/Kinesthetic Visual Auditory	Bodily/Kinesthetic Interpersonal Visual/Spatial Intrapersonal
Word Diagrams	Tactile/Kinesthetic Visual	Bodily/Kinesthetic Interpersonal Visual/Spatial Intrapersonal
Circling Words	Tactile/Kinesthetic Visual Auditory	Visual/Spatial Interpersonal Musical/Rhythmic
Word Sort	Tactile/Kinesthetic Visual Auditory	Visual/Spatial Intrapersonal

Anglo-Saxon Vocabulary

The lessons that follow illustrate the influences that other languages have had on English. Most of the lessons are like puzzles that the students need to solve.

Before the Norman invasion in 1066, the Angles and Saxons ruled. Despite the influences of foreign words, over 25 percent of our English vocabulary comes from the language of the Angles and Saxons. Many of our basic words are of Anglo-Saxon origin, as shown in Exhibit 6.2. In studying word origins, students learn more about our language and add to their growing vocabulary. The more students know about vocabulary, the more they can improve reading comprehension. See the handouts in Exhibits 6.3 and 6.4.

Exhibit 6.2   Anglo-Saxon Vocabulary

Anglo-Saxon Vocabulary

Objectives	To expose students to words and word parts that originated from the Anglo-Saxons.
Materials	Anglo-Saxon Vocabulary Handouts (Exhibits 6.3 and 6.4)
Time	30–40 minutes

Procedure

Step 1	Make copies of the accompanying handouts and explain to students about the impact that other foreign languages can have on a language.
Step 2	Divide the class into groups of four to discuss and complete the handout.
Step 3	Once the students have completed the handout, discuss in a large group and use the following questions and prompts: What did you learn about language? What words could you add to the lists? Why do you think these words have remained in English?
IRA/NCTE Standards	**6.** Students apply knowledge of language structure, language conventions (e.g., spelling and punctuation), media techniques, figurative language, and genre to create, critique, and discuss print and non-print texts.

Exhibit 6.3 Anglo-Saxon Handout 1 (Prefixes)

Word	Meaning
A:	*on, in, at*
Aboard	on a ship, train, or bus
Afoul	in collision
Aloof	at or from a distance, withdrawn, apart
Abed	
Adrift	
Afield	
Afloat	
Aloft	
with:	*against, back*
Withdraw	draw back, take back
Withhold	hold back
Withstand	stand against, resist
be:	*all around, on all sides*
Beset	attack on all sides, surround
Begrudge	
Belabor	
Bemuddle	
Besiege	
Besmirch	
be:	*affect with, cover with*
Begrime	cover with grime, make dirty
Becloud	
Bedevil	
Befog	
Belie	
Bewitch	
be:	*cause to be*
Belittle	cause to be little or unimportant
Becalm	
Bewilder	

Exhibit 6.4   Anglo-Saxon Handout 2 (Suffixes)

Word	Meaning
wise:	*way, manner*
breadthwise	
lengthwise	
otherwise	
dom:	*dignity, office, realm, state of being, those having the characteristic of*
earldom	realm of an earl
martyrdom	state of being a martyr
dukedom	
serfdom	
sheikdom	
some:	*having a considerable degree of the quality denoted in the first part of some word.*
cumbersome	full of encumbrances, stifling
fulsome	offensive because of an excessive display of insincerity
mettlesome	full of mettle, or courage
noisome	offensive to the sense of smell
winsome	full of winning quality, merry
bothersome	
fearsome	
frolicsome	
gruesome	
quarrelsome	
some:	*group of*
twosome	group of two
threesome	
ling:	*one pertaining to or concerned with whatever is denoted in the first part of the word*
hireling	one who receives pay for work performed
starveling	one who is thin from lack of food
yearling	
ling:	*little*
duckling	little duck
gosling	
sapling	

148

Invading Words

The English language is filled with words that come from different languages. When Britain was invaded by the Normans in 1066, the invading army, led by William the Conqueror, brought their language as well—Norman-French. As a result, many words that are part of our modern English were introduced almost one thousand years ago. See Exhibit 6.5 for a lesson plan.

As discussed earlier, the origins of words add to students' growing vocabulary. Not only did the Anglo-Saxons influence our language, but the Norman-French and Scandinavians did as well. Katie regularly shared the handouts in Exhibits 6.6 through 6.8 with her eleventh-grade British literature students so that they could see the foreign influences on the English language.

Exhibit 6.5   Invading Words Lesson Plan

Invading Words Lesson

Objective	To expose students to words and word parts that originated from the Normans
Materials	Norman-French Vocabulary
Time	30–40 minutes

Procedure

Step 1	Make enough copies of the handout for all of the students. Put the students in groups of four to complete the handout. Give the students the following direction: Explain about the Norman invasion of Britain in 1066 and how this affected our language. Instruct the students that they are now language detectives, and that with what they will learn about Norman-French and what they already know about English, they are to see what patterns emerge and what words became part of the English vocabulary.
Step 2	The students will work in their groups to complete the accompanying handout.
Step 3	When the students complete the handout, hold a large-group discussion about what they observed about the language patterns.
IRA/NCTE Standards	**6.** Students apply knowledge of language structure, language conventions (e.g., spelling and punctuation), media techniques, figurative language, and genre to create, critique, and discuss print and non-print texts.

Exhibit 6.6   Invading Words Handout: Word Set 1

Look at the words in Norman-French and compare them to the Anglo-Saxon list. What connection is there between these words?

Norman-French	Anglo-Saxon
beef	cow
mutton	sheep
pork	pig

Prior to the 1066 invasion, the words had the same meaning in these different languages. How are these words similar and different?

Word connection:

Exhibit 6.7   Invading Words Handout: Word Set 2

Anglo-Saxon	English
close	shut
reply	answer
odour	smell
annual	yearly
demand	ask
chamber	room
desire	wish
power	might
ire	wrath/anger

What is the relationship between these words?
Word connection:

Teaching the Classics in the Inclusive Classroom

Exhibit 6.8 Invading Words Handout: Word Set 3

Before the invasion in 1066, Scandinavian tribes influenced Anglo-Saxon English.

Norse	English
anger	wrath
nay	no
fro	from
raise	rear
ill	sick
bask	bathe
skill	craft
skin	hide
dike	ditch
skirt	shirt
scatter	shatter
skip	shift

What is the relationship between these words?
Word connection:

Words in Action

This next lesson is a staple in our classrooms. Students enjoy the creative challenge of creating dramatic interpretations. See Exhibit 6.9 for a lesson plan.

Exhibit 6.9   Words in Action Lesson Plan

Words in Action

Objectives	To interpret, physicalize, and represent word meanings
Materials	Selected words written on pieces of paper or index cards and placed in a box or jar
Time	30–40 minutes

Procedure

Step 1	This activity runs more smoothly when the students work collaboratively in groups of three.
Step 2	Each group of students should select a word and rehearse the meaning of the word. It should take the groups about 2–3 minutes to prepare.
Step 3	Each group will present their dramatization of their assigned word and the other groups can guess the meaning.
IRA/NCTE Standards	**6.** Students apply knowledge of language structure, language conventions (e.g., spelling and punctuation), media techniques, figurative language, and genre to create, critique, and discuss print and non-print texts.

The word diagram lesson plan in Exhibit 6.10 requires students to examine word origins and meanings. This understanding must be internalized so that they are able to physicalize and represent the word. The kinesthetic aspects of this lesson are designed expressly for students to internalize the vocabulary they are learning.

When students do not understand an author's vocabulary, as is the case in many of the literature classics, they face obstacles in comprehension. As discussed earlier, good vocabulary instruction introduces useful and important words that enhance understanding of a text. With frequent exposure to the vocabulary, students are more likely to include the new words in their personal vocabulary. The diagrams in Figures 6.1 and 6.2 promote students' understanding of word origins, relationships between words, and word structures. The circling words lesson in Exhibit 6.11 offers a tool for teaching specific vocabulary words.

Exhibit 6.10 Word Diagram Lesson Plan

Word Diagrams

Objective	To examine word meanings and origins
Materials	Plain paper, markers, crayons, colored pencils. A hat, a box, or another container where the teacher can deposit the words that are to be used for this assignment
Time	20–30 minutes in class or good as homework

Procedure

Step 1	Copy the accompanying handout and distribute to the students. Create a model for the students so that they have something that they can refer to when they create their own.
Step 2	The students should draw a word from those that the teacher pre-selected and complete the word diagram.
Step 3	Once the word diagrams are complete the students should be grouped in pairs or trios to discuss their pictures. What did the students find challenging to do in the word diagrams? What did they learn from completing this activity?
IRA/NCTE Standards	**6.** Students apply knowledge of language structure, language conventions (e.g., spelling and punctuation), media techniques, figurative language, and genre to create, critique, and discuss print and non-print texts.

Figure 6.1   Word Diagram Template

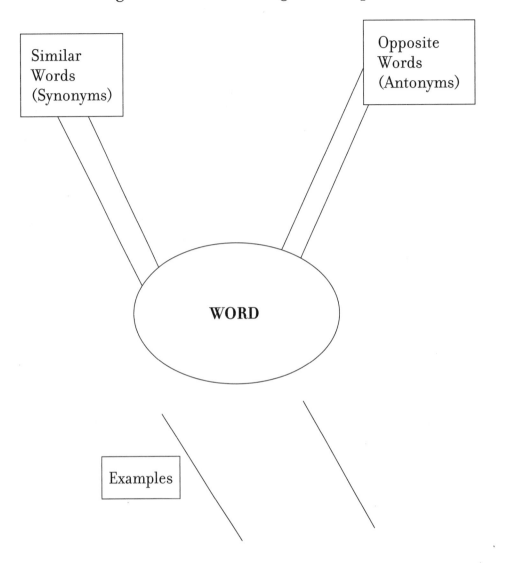

Similar Words (Synonyms)

Opposite Words (Antonyms)

WORD

Examples

QUOTE OR SEGMENT THAT CONTAINS THE VOCABULARY WORD

_____

_____

_____

_____

_____

Figure 6.2 Sample Word Diagram

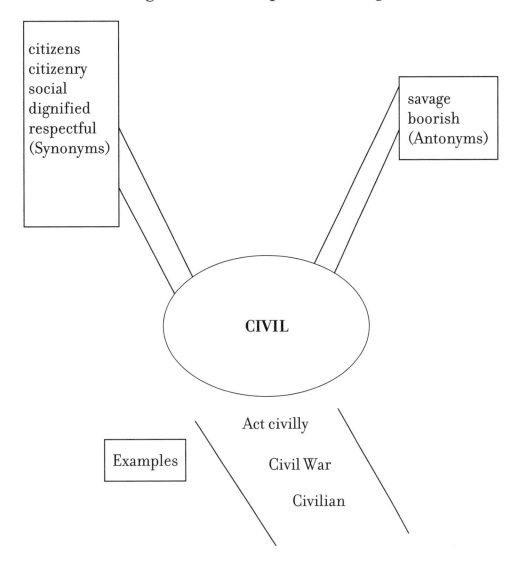

citizens
citizenry
social
dignified
respectful
(Synonyms)

savage
boorish
(Antonyms)

CIVIL

Examples

Act civilly

Civil War

Civilian

QUOTE OR SEGMENT THAT CONTAINS THE VOCABULARY WORD

From the prologue of Romeo and Juliet, Line 4, "Civil blood makes civil hands unclean." Citizens dirty their hands by their violence against fellow citizens," as in "civil war."

Exhibit 6.11   Circling Words Lesson Plan

Circling Words

Objectives	To develop comprehension of specific vocabulary
Materials	A list of vocabulary words and definitions written on index cards
Time	20 minutes

Procedure

Step 1	It's more effective if the students randomly select words from a teacher-generated list. Once the students have a selected word, they should write the definition on the other side. One side has the word, and the other has the definition.
Step 2	Have the students stand and create two concentric circles — one inside the other. The students in the inside circle turn around to face the students in the outside circle.
Step 3	The students should face each other and the teacher calls "Inside!" or "Outside!" The called circle gives the student that they are facing their word or definition. Their partner must give the definition or the word in response. Once the students complete their exchange, the teacher calls "rotate" and the circles move. The teacher then calls "stop" and there is a new pair. The circles stop and move so that there are new pairings. Every student practices vocabulary and repeats words for greater reinforcement.
IRA/NCTE Standards	**6.** Students apply knowledge of language structure, language conventions (e.g., spelling and punctuation), media techniques, figurative language, and genre to create, critique, and discuss print and non-print texts.

Teaching the Classics in the Inclusive Classroom

Word Sort

The activity in Exhibit 6.12 emphasizes word structures and relationships, which are key components of good vocabulary instruction. This word sort lesson builds on students' innate understanding of language, and its kinesthetic elements tap into the multiple intelligences of different kinds of learners. Exhibit 6.13 presents word sorts for *Jane Eyre*, and Exhibit 6.14 shows word sorts for *Pride and Prejudice*.

Tips

- Purchase business cards at an office supply store. Print the lists on the business card sheets and place them in envelopes.

- Print each group's list in a separate color so you can keep better track of complete word-sort sets.

Exhibit 6.12 Word Sort Lesson Plan

Word Sort

Objective	To build on innate understanding of language to sort vocabulary words
Materials	Index cards, markers
Time	20–40 minutes, depending on list

Procedure

Step 1	Some sample word lists are included. The students should be divided into groups of three or four students, so you should make a set of word cards for each group.
Step 2	In their groups, the students should sort the word cards. They can use categories like parts of speech, synonyms, antonyms. The students may use a dictionary.
Step 3	Once the students have categorized their words, they can discuss them as a large group and attempt to make one word sort list for the entire class. At the end of the activity, ask the students, "What did you learn and why is it important?"
IRA/NCTE Standards	**6.** Students apply knowledge of language structure, language conventions (e.g., spelling and punctuation), media techniques, figurative language, and genre to create, critique, and discuss print and non-print texts.

Teaching the Classics in the Inclusive Classroom

Exhibit 6.13 Word Sort List for *Jane Eyre*

Chapters 1–10

morose	sequester	turbulent	antagonist	kindling	pendant	pervade
simultaneously	obliterate	usurious	frock	engender	pinafore	retaliation
transient	mastiff	apothecary	synonymous	degradation	ire	apparel
pungent	bellow	garter	ignominy	browbeaten	conjecture	wretchedness
promotion	vignette	gallows	infliction	captious	insolent	peremptory
veranda	ruddy	gradation	penurious	perfidious	repugnance	tresses
refectory	luster	fervid	pestilence	consumption	solace	

Chapters 11–20

impediment	venerable	relic	prattle	stagnation	rookery	dispose
grimace	brooch	physiognomy	condole	propitious	novice	portfolio
suffusion	affability	philanthropist	haughty	gregarious	inopportune	pique
insolence	resolute	innate	fallible	coquetry	gnome	consecrate
destitute	stupefy	vex	equestrian	countenance	thwart	blunder
scrutiny	susceptible	pungent	volatile	insipid	beguile	anathema
enigma	adhere	juncture	inflammatory	grimace	chagrin	multitudinous

Chapters 21–30

expedient	smote	coercion	feign	ardent	insufferable	revile
garb	oblivion	impediment	perverse	sneer	insolvency	noxious
remonstrance	repel	lattice	genial	morass	aperture	omnipotence
skepticism	exultation	sprite	stile	gossamer	asperity	specter
predominate	ascetic	lethargic	frivolous	indolence	entreat	fastidious

Chapters 31–38

warp	intractable	relinquish	impropriety	indulgent	reconcilement	gnaw
clad	insatiable	assiduous	repast	oculist	chastisement	infallible
austerity	bequest	scrupulous	doleful	conjecture	incredulous	annihilation
despotic	tenacious	enunciation	priggish	beneficent	lacerate	surmise
vivacity	pithy					

Exhibit 6.14   Word Sort List for *Pride and Prejudice*

Chapters 1–21

impertinent	fortnight	indignation	insipid	draught	countenance	assent
eminent	stout	prevail	odious	deceitful	expostulation	reprehensible
infinite	civility	novelty	willful	propitious	felicity	rectory
amends	deference	affability	abode	tête à tête	parsonage	deign
contemplation	esteem	degenerate	proxy	procure	probity	exultation
humility	discernment	bestow	insolent	persevere	injunction	patroness
condescend	coquetry					

Chapters 21–40

abound	simpleton	desponding	solicitation	trifle	composure	incredulous
boisterous	rapturous	abhorrence	inclination	circumspect	canvass	solemnity
perverse	entail	thwart	assert	duplicity	defection	conciliate
alacrity	indisposed	controverted	sally	derive	peruse	impute
avowal	endeavor	remorse	suppress	disapprobation	verdure	refute
pecuniary	encumbrance	insolence	perusal	profligate	benevolence	contrivance
approbation	fervent	affront	vindication			

Chapters 41–50

lamentation	vexation	frivolous	impute	impropriety	acquiesce
bestow	perverse	cordiality	tincture	repugnant	impetuous
consolatory	elopement	lamentation	villainous	fretful	infamy
dilatory	sanguine	licentiousness	conjecture	exuberance	folly
connubial	felicity				

Chapters 51–60

vestibule	abash	impertinence	scruple
inducement	sedate	vex	dupe
pretension	incessant	sagacity	closure

Teaching the Classics in the Inclusive Classroom

Graphic Organizers

Graphic organizers are useful tools for teaching vocabulary because they help students organize and visualize what they are learning. All students benefit from graphic organizers, because the activity employs several different intelligences and aids in the study of language and vocabulary. Remember that at the beginning of this chapter we asserted that vocabulary should be studied and not memorized. There are many resources for graphic organizers, and from the array we have selected a few that we like and believe are particularly useful for students with special needs. Figures 6.3, 6.4, 6.5, and 6.6 offer graphic organizers that are useful for teaching vocabulary.

Ten More Vocabulary Activities

1. *Sticky Notes.* Use these while reading. Students can record unfamiliar words and develop definitions based on the context from their reading.

2. *Words Walls.* This strategy is often considered for younger students, but adolescent students benefit as well. The students can select words to contribute to the word wall, which should be displayed in the classroom. Pictures can be added to the words to convey the meaning. A multimodal display like this is particularly beneficial for students with special needs.

3. *Vocabulary Self-Selection.* Students select unfamiliar words from their reading and compile them in a journal or dictionary. Encourage students to draw pictures and experiment with the words in their writing.

4. *Vocabulary Cartoons.* Have the students pick words from a prepared vocabulary list (probably one for a novel or literature unit). The students can draw a one-to-three-frame cartoon that reflects and teaches the meaning of the vocabulary.

5. *Picture Dictionary.* Have students draw illustrations of vocabulary words and bind them in a personal book or a classroom dictionary.

6. *Word-of-the-Day.* Similar to the calendars, the students can bring a word of the day in for the students to discuss and display in the classroom.

7. *Word Games.* Bring in games that students can play.

8. *Crossword Puzzles and Word Searches.* These are great tools for students to learn new words. Several Internet sites allow teachers to create custom word puzzles.

9. *Internet Sites.* The following sites teach students about vocabulary.

    1. http://www.freevocabulary.com (contains over 5,000 words that students can study for college entrance examinations).

    2. http://grammar.ccc.commnet.edu/grammar/vocabulary.htm (a vocabulary-building Web site, with quizzes and interesting information about word roots and origins).

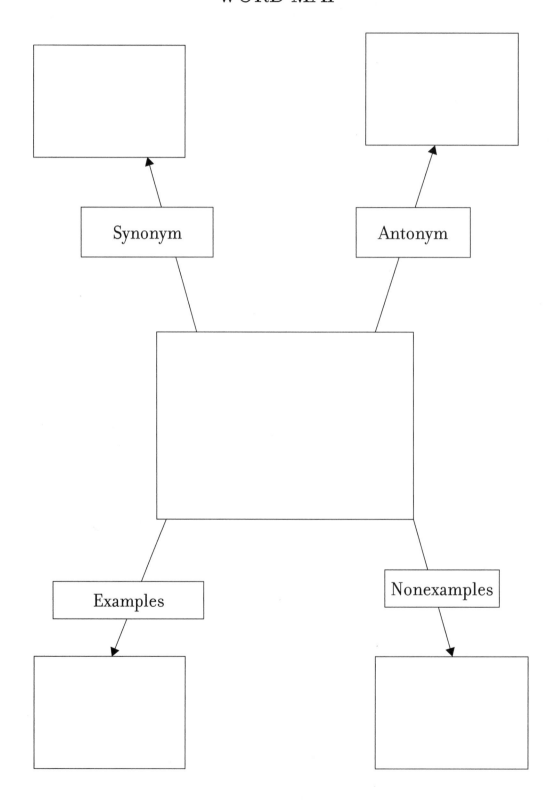

Figure 6.3 Word Map Template

WORD MAP

Synonym

Antonym

Examples

Nonexamples

Figure 6.4 Word Detective Template

WORD DETECTIVE

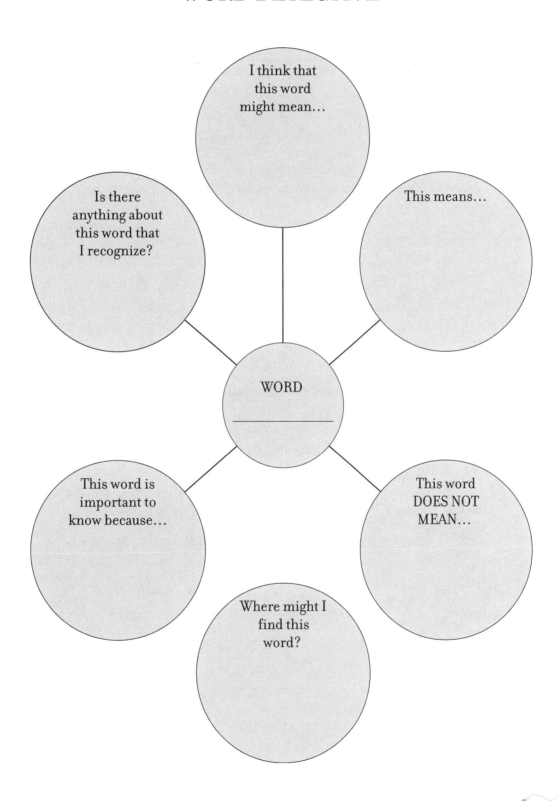

Figure 6.5   Word Chain Template

SYNONYM   SYNONYM

TARGET
WORD

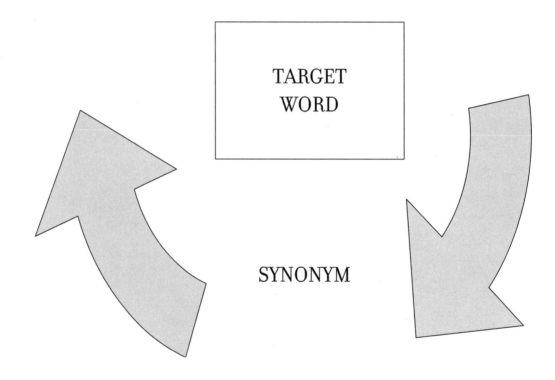

SYNONYM

Figure 6.6   Contextual Word Map Template

LOOKING AT WORDS IN CONTEXT

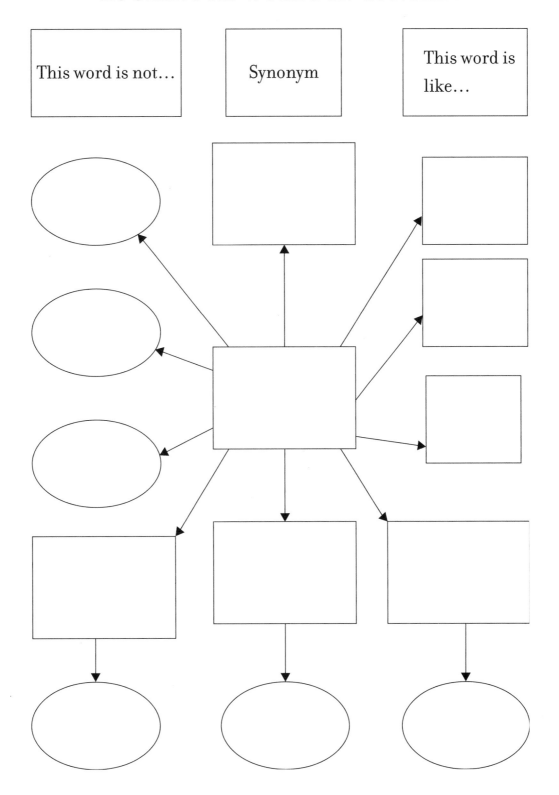

3. http://www.englishonline.net/word.html (a word-a-day Web site that students can visit).

4. http://www.superkids.com/aweb/tools/words/hangman/sat1.shtml (play hangman with college entrance exam words; college entrance exam vocabulary tests are composed of words commonly found in the literature classics).

10. *Bingo Games.* Use the vocabulary words and definitions as a pre-reading activity.

Teaching the Classics in the Inclusive Classroom

Part Two

Working with Selected Classic Texts

Chapter Seven

Putting the Strategies into Action

After much consideration, we decided not to offer suggested timelines for the instructional plans because classrooms always differ. One class could complete *Romeo and Juliet* in five weeks, and another might take longer. The teacher in the classroom knows the students better than anyone else and can better judge the time that activities will take.

The purpose of this chapter is to illustrate direct applications of the strategies that are outlined in the previous chapters.

Instructional Plan for Teaching *Romeo and Juliet* to All Students

Pre-Reading

Anticipation Guides. As described in Chapter Two, the students make predictions about the text in anticipation guides. A full anticipation guide for all five acts of *Romeo and Juliet* is included here.

During Reading

Character Diaries and Character Bookmarks. Promoting student connections and engagement with canonical literature can be challenging. Both of these writing activities promote personal connections, as the students step into the role of a character that they selected from a text.

Character Bookmarks. Keeping all those characters straight in a Dickens novel is never easy. Templates and student samples of bookmarks are included for *Romeo and Juliet*.

After Reading

Making Memories. This scrapbooking activity, as described in Chapter Four, is designed to promote visualization and extend students' understanding of the play. Templates, suggested pages, and guidelines for *Romeo and Juliet* are shared.

Pre-Reading Anticipation Guide for *Romeo and Juliet*

Act 1, Scene 1   Before you read, predict which of the statements about scene 1 is accurate. Write *Yes* in the "before" column if you predict the statement to be accurate. As you read scene 1, write *Yes* in the "after" column if the play proves the statement and *No* if the play disproves the statement. In the line numbers column, write the number of the line(s) on which you found the answer.

Synopsis. The action in *Romeo and Juliet* occurs over a five-day period. It is Sunday morning in the public street in Verona, Italy.

Teaching the Classics in the Inclusive Classroom

Before: Yes or No		After: Yes or No	Line Number(s)
	Sampson and Gregory are Capulets' servants.		
	Sampson says he refuses to excuse insults.		
	Sampson expects insults from the Montague servants.		
	Abraham and Balthazar are Montague's servants.		
	Sampson bites his thumb at Abraham and Balthasar. This is an insulting gesture.		
	The servants fight with insults, not swords.		
	Benvolio is Capulets' nephew and Juliet's cousin.		
	Benvolio enthusiastically joins the sword fight.		
	Tybalt is Montague's nephew and Romeo's cousin.		
	Tybalt loves peace, hell, Montagues, and Benvolio.		
	Another sword fight begins. Members of the Capulet and Montague families join the fight.		
	Lady Capulet tells her husband that he is too old to fight.		
	Lady Montague encourages her husband to fight.		
	In lines 56–78, Prince Escalus criticizes both houses for having three street fights and sentences anyone who engages in more street fights to death.		
	Everyone leaves the street except Lord and Lady Montague and Benvolio.		
	In lines 81–90, Benvolio tells his aunt and uncle a lie about the street fight.		
	In lines 94–105, Benvolio says that Romeo was out walking an hour before dawn.		
	Lord Montague wonders why his son shuts out the daylight and prefers to be outside at night.		

Act 1, Scene 2

Before: Yes or No		After: Yes or No	Line Number(s)
	Capulet and Paris, relatives of Prince Escalus, discuss the latest street fight.		
	Paris says he wishes to marry Capulet's daughter, Juliet.		
	Capulet likes Paris, and vows to force Juliet to marry him even if she doesn't want to.		
	Capulet sends a servant to invite guests to a party to be held in Paris's honor.		
	Benvolio and Romeo meet Capulet, Paris, and the servant in the street.		
	Romeo reads the guest list and sees that Rosaline, the girl he loves, is an invited guest.		
	After the servant leaves, Benvolio encourages Romeo to crash the Capulets' party in order to meet another girl who makes him forget about Rosaline.		
	Romeo refuses to attend any party given by a Capulet.		
	When Romeo enters the street, the stage directions explain the reason for his depression.		
	Romeo admits to Benvolio, his cousin, that he loves a girl who does not return his love.		
	Romeo describes unreturned love in opposites or oxymorons, such as "loving hate," "heavy lightness," "bright smoke," "cold fire," "sick health," and "waking sleep."		
	Benvolio suggests that Romeo needs to find someone else.		
	Romeo agrees with Benvolio.		
	Benvolio vows to prove to Romeo that Romeo can find someone else.		

At one point in this scene, Sampson and Gregory plan their fight strategy in a whispered conversation that only they and the audience can hear. This conversation is called an *aside*. What information do these servants give in their aside?

Act 2, Scenes 1 and 2 *Romeo and Juliet* takes place in five days; scenes 1 and 2 take place on a Sunday. The setting is outside the Capulet mansion in Verona, Italy. Montague characters are Romeo, Benvolio, and Mercutio; Capulet characters are Juliet and the Nurse.

Before you read the scene, read the following statements. Some of these statements are true, and others are not. As you read each statement, predict whether each statement is true or not. In the "before" column, write *Yes* if you predict the statement is accurate; write *No* if you think the statement is inaccurate.

As you read the play, write *Yes* or *No* in the "after" column if the text proves that the statement is true or not.

Don't forget to read the stage directions!

Act 1, Scenes 1 and 2

Before		After
	Scene 1	
	Benvolio tells Mercutio that Romeo has remained on the Capulets' grounds after the party.	
	Mercutio teases Romeo about Juliet.	
	Mercutio and Benvolio go home and leave Romeo alone in the Capulets' orchard.	
	Scene 2	
	Romeo sees Juliet on the balcony outside her bedroom window as he hides in the trees below.	
	Romeo says Juliet is the sun.	
	Juliet says she wishes she and Romeo had other last names.	
	When Juliet says that "a rose by any other name would smell as sweet," she means that Romeo would be the same person if he was not a Montague.	

Juliet makes a speech that the audience can hear. This is referred to as a *soliloquy*. What does Juliet reveal in this speech?

Act 3, Scene 1 Before you read the scene, read the following statements. Some of these statements are true, and others are not. As you read each statement, predict whether each statement is true or not. In the "before" column, write *Yes* if you predict the statement is accurate; write *No* if you think the statement is inaccurate.

As you read the play, write *Yes* or *No* on the "after" column if the text proves that the statement is true or not.

Don't forget to read the stage directions!

Act 3, Scene 1

Before		After
	Benvolio wants a fight with the Capulets.	
	Mercutio accuses Benvolio of being ready to fight over unimportant things.	
	Mercutio tells Tybalt that he would like to talk and fight with him.	
	Tybalt's purpose when he meets Benvolio and Mercutio is to ask them if they are friends with Romeo.	
	Benvolio suggests that they go somewhere less public than the street and "reason" rather than fight over their differences.	
	Mercutio agrees that he wants to go somewhere private.	
	When Romeo enters, Mercutio tells Tybalt that Romeo will meet Tybalt at a dueling field to fight.	
	Tybalt insults Romeo.	
	Tybalt challenges Romeo to a duel.	
	Romeo says he loves the Capulet name and refuses a fight.	
	Mercutio insults Tybalt and challenges him to a duel. Mercutio then draws his sword.	

Teaching the Classics in the Inclusive Classroom

Act 3, Scene 1 cont.

Before		After
	Mercutio compliments Tybalt when he calls him "Good King of Cats" and asks him for one of his nine lives.	
	Mercutio says he is hurt and will be dead or a "grave" man by tomorrow. Mercutio forgives Tybalt.	
	Mercutio blames Romeo for coming between him and Tybalt and tells Romeo he was stabbed under Romeo's arm.	
	In a soliloquy, Romeo says his love for Juliet has made him feminine.	
	Benvolio tells Romeo that Mercutio will recover.	
	Benvolio tells Romeo to run away since the Prince is coming.	
	Lady Capulet pleads for Romeo's life from the Prince.	
	Lord Montague says that there has been enough killing and that the Prince should spare Romeo's life.	

Predict what you think will happen in the next scene.

Act 3, Scene 2   Before you read the scene, read the following statements. Some of these statements are true, and others are not. As you read each statement, predict whether each statement is true or not. In the "before" column, write *Yes* if you predict the statement is accurate; write *No* if you think the statement is inaccurate.

As you read the play, write *Yes* or *No* in the "after" column if the text proves that the statement is true or not.

Don't forget to read the stage directions!

It is Monday afternoon, immediately after the deaths of Mercutio and Tybalt. The scene takes place in the Capulets' orchard.

Act 3, Scene 2

Before		After
	Juliet reveals in her soliloquy that she is impatient for the night to come.	
	Juliet compliments Romeo when she wishes that he be cut into stars to decorate the heavens after he dies.	
	Juliet realizes that Tybalt is dead and Romeo banished.	
	When the Nurse repeats "he's dead," Juliet assumes that the Nurse is referring to Romeo.	
	The Nurse hated Tybalt when he was alive.	
	Juliet says she is happy to hear of the death of Tybalt, her hated cousin.	
	Juliet forgives Romeo for killing her cousin.	
	Juliet admits that since one of them had to die, she is relieved it is Tybalt and not Romeo.	
	Juliet tells the Nurse that she feels much worse than Lord and Lady Capulet who are weeping for Tybalt.	
	Juliet sends the Nurse to find Romeo.	

Act 3, Scene 3 Before you read the scene, read the following statements. Some of these statements are true, and others are not. As you read each statement, predict whether each statement is true or not. In the "before" column, write *Yes* if you predict the statement is accurate; write *No* if you think the statement is inaccurate.

As you read the play, write *Yes* or *No* on the "after" column if the text proves that the statement is true or not.

Don't forget to read the stage directions!

The setting is on Monday afternoon in Friar Laurence's cell in Verona, Italy.

Teaching the Classics in the Inclusive Classroom

Act 3, Scene 3

Before		After
	Romeo does not learn of his banishment until he is told of it by Friar Laurence.	
	Romeo is relieved to be sent outside Verona's walls.	
	Friar Laurence believes that banishment is kind.	
	Romeo believes banishment is death.	
	Friar Laurence is able to calm Romeo before the Nurse enters.	
	Friar Laurence tells the Nurse that Romeo is crying.	
	The Nurse says that Juliet is weeping as well.	
	Romeo is sure that Juliet does not blame him for killing Tybalt.	
	Romeo draws his dagger to kill himself.	
	Friar Laurence loses his temper with Romeo and calls him womanish.	
	Friar Laurence assures the Nurse that Romeo will be coming to visit Juliet at the Capulet house that night.	
	The Nurse takes Romeo's ring to give to Juliet.	
	Friar Laurence tells Romeo to go to Mantua, an Italian city about 20 miles from Verona.	

Act 3, Scenes 4 and 5 Before you read the scenes, read the following statements. Some of these statements are true, and others are not. As you read each statement, predict whether each statement is true or not. In the "before" column, write *Yes* if you predict the statement is accurate; write *No* if you think the statement is inaccurate.

As you read the play, write *Yes* or *No* on the "after" column if the text proves that the statement is true or not.

Don't forget to read the stage directions!

The action of scene 4 takes place on Monday night at the Capulets' house.

The setting of scene 5 is the balcony outside Juliet's bedroom, which overlooks the Capulets' orchard.

Before		After
	Lady Capulet promises Paris that she will learn tomorrow if Juliet wishes to many him.	
	Lord Capulet, however, decides to give Juliet to Paris without asking Juliet.	
	Lord Capulet instructs his wife to tell Juliet that their daughter will marry Paris.	
	At first, Lord Capulet sets Wednesday as the wedding day for Juliet and Paris.	
	Lord Capulet says that the wedding will be a wonderful and happy affair.	
	Capulet instructs his wife to tell Juliet about the upcoming marriage the next morning.	
	Romeo will be executed if he is caught in Verona after sunrise.	
	Juliet feels now that Romeo should leave for Mantua at once.	
	Romeo says that he will stay since he has a greater desire to stay than leave.	
	Juliet has decided Romeo must leave immediately.	
	The Nurse does not warn Juliet that her mother is coming to her bedroom.	
	Romeo leaves Juliet's bedroom on a rope ladder.	
	Juliet foreshadows her own death.	
	Romeo tells Juliet that she, like her new husband, is pale as death.	
	In a soliloquy, Juliet begs fortune to return to her and Romeo.	
	Lady Capulet believes that Juliet has spent the night weeping for Tybalt.	
	Lady Capulet speaks well of Romeo.	
	In an aside, Juliet tells the Nurse that Romeo is not a villain.	
	Lady Capulet has a scheme to poison Romeo even though she believes that he is already in exile in Mantua.	

Act 3, Scene 5

Before		After
	Juliet tells her mother that she will never cooperate in her plan to poison Romeo.	
	Lady Capulet states that Juliet's considerate father has chosen to make a surprising day of joy to help Juliet forget the grief of Tybalt.	
	Juliet agrees to her father's plans.	
	Lady Capulet is at first surprised by Juliet's refusal to marry Paris.	
	Juliet tells her father that she is thankful for his love although she hates the idea of marrying Paris.	
	Although Juliet begs on her knees, Lord Capulet refuses to change his mind.	
	The Nurse supports Lady Capulet.	
	Lord Capulet threatens to send Juliet out of the house to "hang, beg, starve, and die in the streets" unless she marries Paris.	
	Lady Capulet agrees to help her daughter.	
	After Lord Capulet leaves, Juliet begs her mother to delay the wedding.	
	After Lady Capulet leaves, Juliet begs the Nurse for help.	
	The Nurse says that since Romeo is banished forever, Juliet should marry Paris.	
	Juliet sends the Nurse to Lady Capulet with the message that Juliet will go to confession in Friar Laurence's cell. Juliet claims that she wants to confess the sin of disobedience to her father.	
	Juliet reveals in her soliloquy that she will never forgive the Nurse and will seek help from Friar Laurence.	
	If Friar Laurence fails her, Juliet vows to run away to Mantua.	

Act 4, Scene 1   Before you read the scene, read the following statements. Some of these statements are true, and others are not. As you read each statement, predict whether each statement is true or not. In the "before" column, write *Yes* if you predict the statement is accurate; write *No* if you think the statement is inaccurate.

As you read the play, write *Yes* or *No* on the "after" column if the text proves that the statement is true or not.

Don't forget to read the stage directions!

The scene takes place at Friar Laurence's cell on Tuesday morning.

Act 4, Scene 1

Before		After
	Paris tells Friar Laurence that he is eager to help Romeo and Juliet.	
	Paris explains that Lord Capulet's reason for setting the date for the marriage so soon is to stop Juliet's mourning for her cousin Tybalt.	
	Friar Laurence tells Paris in an aside that he wishes that he did not know why the proposed marriage should be delayed.	
	Juliet enters the cell after Paris leaves.	
	When Juliet says "What must be shall be," this is an example of foreshadowing.	
	Paris speaks of Juliet's face as his and she replies it is "not mine own." This is an example of irony because she and Friar Laurence know her face belongs to Romeo and Paris assumes it is his.	
	Friar Laurence asks Paris to leave so he can hear Juliet's confession.	
	Juliet tells Friar Laurence that she will stab herself to death if he cannot help her.	
	Friar Laurence tells Juliet that he will give her a "thing like death" to escape marrying Paris.	

Act 4, Scene 1 cont.

Before		After
	Friar Laurence tells Juliet to drink a vial of liquor on Wednesday night. This liquor will make her pulse stop, make her cold to the touch, slow her breathing, and make her appear dead.	
	Friar Laurence claims that Juliet will wake up in the Capulet vault to find Romeo.	

Act 4, Scene 2   Before you read the scene, read the following statements. Some of these statements are true, and others are not. As you read each statement, predict if each statement is true or not. In the ''before'' column, write *Yes* if you predict the statement is accurate; write *No* if you think the statement is inaccurate.

     As you read the play, write *Yes* or *No* in the ''after'' column if the text proves that the statement is true or not.

     Don't forget to read the stage directions!

     The scene takes place Tuesday afternoon in the Capulets' home.

Act 4, Scene 2

Before		After
	Lord Capulet shows that he is no longer angry at Juliet for refusing to marry Paris.	
	Juliet enters and apologizes to her father for her disobedience and tells her father that she will marry Paris.	
	Juliet and the Nurse exit to find Paris and tell him that the marriage will take place.	

Act 4, Scene 3   Before you read the scene, read the following statements. Some of these statements are true, and others are not. As you read each statement, predict whether each statement is true or not. In the ''before'' column, write *Yes* if you predict the statement is accurate; write *No* if you think the statement is inaccurate.

     As you read the play, write *Yes* or *No* in the ''after'' column if the text proves that the statement is true or not.

     Don't forget to read the stage directions!

     The action continues in the Capulets' home.

Act 4, Scene 3

Before		After
	Lady Capulet enters Juliet's chamber briefly and then leaves the Nurse to make last-minute wedding preparations.	
	Juliet feels no fear before drinking the vial that Friar Laurence has given her.	
	Juliet lays a dagger near her bed in case the potion does not work and she must marry Paris.	
	Juliet trusts the Friar completely.	
	Juliet fears she will awake in the family tomb and die there before Romeo arrives.	
	Juliet drinks the potion that Friar Laurence gave her.	

Act 4, Scene 4   Before you read the scene, read the following statements. Some of these statements are true, and others are not. As you read each statement, predict whether each statement is true or not. In the "before" column, write *Yes* if you predict the statement is accurate; write *No* if you think the statement is inaccurate.

As you read the play, write *Yes* or *No* in the "after" column if the text proves that the statement is true or not.

Don't forget to read the stage directions!

The action continues at the Capulets' home.

Act 4, Scene 4

Before		After
	The Nurse accuses Lord Capulet of meddling in woman's work like cooking.	
	Lord Capulet calls to the Nurse to let Juliet sleep longer.	

Act 4, Scene 5   Before you read the scene, read the following statements. Some of these statements are true and others are not. As you read each statement, predict if each statement is true or not. In the "before" column, write *Yes* if you predict the statement is accurate; write *No* if you think the statement is inaccurate.

As you read the play, write *Yes* or *No* in the "after" column if the text proves that the statement is true or not.

Don't forget to read the stage directions!

Teaching the Classics in the Inclusive Classroom

The action continues at the Capulets' home, in Juliet's bedroom.

Act 4, Scene 5

Before		After
	The Nurse believes that Juliet is dead.	
	Paris enters Juliet's bedchamber when she does not awaken.	
	Friar Laurence tells the Capulets that Juliet is now in heaven.	
	Lord Capulet says that the wedding is now a funeral.	
	Everyone leaves Juliet's bedroom except for the Nurse, who weeps.	

Act 5, Scene 1 Before you read the scene, read the following statements. Some of these statements are true, and others are not. As you read each statement, predict whether each statement is true or not. In the "before" column, write *Yes* if you predict the statement is accurate; write *No* if you think the statement is inaccurate.

As you read the play, write *Yes* or *No* in the "after" column if the text proves that the statement is true or not.

Don't forget to read the stage directions!

The scene takes place on a street in Mantua, Italy.

Act 5, Scene 1

Before		After
	Romeo tells the audience about a happy dream that he had on Wednesday night.	
	Balthasar is the messenger sent by Friar Laurence to tell Romeo about the plan to keep Juliet from marriage to Paris.	
	Balthazar tells Romeo that Juliet's dead body lies in the Capulet tomb.	
	Balthasar says that he rode from Verona to tell Romeo about Juliet's death because Romeo left him the duty to keep him informed about Juliet.	
	Romeo tells Balthasar to rent horses since Romeo is going to Verona that night.	

Act 5, Scenes 1 cont.

Before		After
	Romeo shares his plans for suicide with the audience.	
	An apothecary in Mantua agrees to sell Romeo poison.	
	Romeo decides that he will drink the poison when he is at Juliet's side.	

Act 5, Scene 2   Before you read the scene, read the following statements. Some of these statements are true, and others are not. As you read each statement, predict whether each statement is true or not. In the "before" column, write *Yes* if you predict the statement is accurate; write *No* if you think the statement is inaccurate.

As you read the play, write *Yes* or *No* in the "after" column if the text proves that the statement is true or not.

Don't forget to read the stage directions!

It is now Thursday at Friar Laurence's cell.

Act 5, Scenes 2

Before		After
	Friar John is another priest who was sent to deliver Friar Laurence's letter about the plan to avoid Juliet's second wedding. Friar John was to have given the letter to Romeo in Mantua.	
	Friar John explains that he went to find another friar to accompany him to Mantua.	
	The Mantua gatekeepers would not let Friar John into the town because they thought that he was sick.	
	Friar John did not deliver the message to Romeo.	

Act 5, Scene 3   Before you read the scene, read the following statements. Some of these statements are true, and others are not. As you read each statement, predict whether each statement is true or not. In the "before" column, write *Yes* if you predict the statement is accurate; write *No* if you think the statement is inaccurate.

As you read the play, write *Yes* or *No* in the "after" column if the text proves that the statement is true or not.

Don't forget to read the stage directions!

Teaching the Classics in the Inclusive Classroom

This scene takes place in the Capulet vault.

Act 5, Scene 3

Before	After
Romeo immediately challenges Paris to a duel.	
Romeo kills Paris.	
Romeo places Paris's body in an empty tomb inside of the Capulets' vault.	
Romeo asks Tybalt for his forgiveness.	
Romeo drinks the poison and dies instantly before he can kiss Juliet.	
Friar Laurence enters the churchyard and meets Balthasar who informs him that Romeo has been in the Capulet vault for a half hour.	
As Friar Laurence discovers Romeo's and Paris's bodies, Juliet awakens.	
Friar Laurence tells Juliet that Romeo and Paris are awaiting her in his cell.	
Friar Laurence tells Juliet to leave with him and he will hide her in a convent of nuns.	
Friar Laurence hears people coming and runs away.	
Juliet tries to get poison from Romeo's lips.	
When Juliet hears the watchmen come, she takes Romeo's dagger and kills herself.	
The watchmen send for the Prince.	
The Capulets, Montagues, and Friar Laurence enter the vault.	
Friar Laurence reveals the truth about Romeo and Juliet.	
The Prince blames the families' hatred for each other for these deaths.	

During Reading

Character Diaries. The character diary activity is fully described in Chapter Five.

Romeo and Juliet Diaries

This activity can take place in class or as a homework assignment.

Objective: To draw personal connections to the main characters. To interpret and analyze a character and its effects on the plot and theme of the play.

Materials: Construction paper, staplers, twine, hole punch, and notebook paper.

Step 1. The students should make a diary using the construction paper for the covers. They can bind them with either a hole punch or stapler.

Step 2. Distribute the accompanying handout and instruct the students to choose either Option A or B.

Step 3. The students can either write in class given or this can be as a homework assignment.

Step 4. Once the students have completed their reading of the play, they can share their diaries with their classmates in small groups. They can compare their diaries and discover how their interpretations of the characters may be similar or different. Another option for sharing the diary entries is to pair off the students and share their entries as Romeo and Juliet.

Character Diary Activity: Romeo and Juliet

Option A

Write a diary for Juliet and include the following entries:

1. Pretend that you are Juliet and write a diary entry that describes Juliet's attitudes and feelings after the second balcony scene with Romeo.
2. Write a second entry while Juliet is waiting for the Nurse to return with Romeo's message.
3. Write a third entry after Juliet hears that Romeo has killed Tybalt.
4. Write a fourth entry after Capulet tells Juliet that she must marry Paris.
5. Write a fifth entry just before Juliet drinks the sleeping potion.

Option B

Write a diary for Romeo and include the following entries:

1. Assume that you are Romeo and write a diary entry that describes your attitudes and feelings after the balcony scene with Juliet.
2. Write a second entry that tells how Romeo felt right after he killed Tybalt.

Teaching the Classics in the Inclusive Classroom

3. Write a third entry that tells how Romeo felt when he was alone in Mantua.

4. Write a fourth entry after Romeo has been told by Balthasar that Juliet is dead.

5. Write a fifth entry right after Romeo killed Paris and before he kills himself.

Character Diary Rubric: Romeo and Juliet

Category	4	3	2	1
Sentences and paragraphs	Sentences and paragraphs are complete, well-constructed, and of varied structure. Content is easily understood because of the sentence structure.	All sentences are complete and well-constructed (no fragments, no run-ons). Content is generally understandable.	Most sentences are complete and well-constructed. Content can be confusing in places due to the sentence structure.	Excessive sentence fragments and run-ons. It is difficult to understand content due to the sentence structure.
Ideas	It was easy to understand the diary entry since the ideas were expressed well and organized logically.	In general, the ideas expressed were clear but better organization could improve the coherence.	Ideas were organized for the most part but it was sometimes difficult to understand the diary entry.	The diary entry seemed to be a collection of unrelated sentences.
Capitalization and punctuation	No errors	1–2 errors	3–4 errors	4 or more errors
Voice	The writer seems to be Romeo or Juliet, and the diary entries are written in first person.	The writer is not consistent as they write as if they are Romeo or Juliet.	The entries are not in first person narrative and the writer does not consistently assume the role of either Romeo or Juliet.	The entries are not in first person narrative and the writer does not assume the role of either Romeo or Juliet.

Character Bookmarks

The character bookmark activity is fully described in Chapter Three.

Objective: To understand the relationships between characters in Shakespeare's *Romeo and Juliet*.

Materials: Construction paper, yarn or string, markers, crayons, colored pencils, hole punch.

Step 1. Explain to the students that they will create bookmarks for *Romeo and Juliet.* The purpose of these bookmarks is to help them keep track of all of the characters in the play. As they read the play, instruct the students to record each character on their bookmark as they encounter them in the play.

Step 2. Give the students half a sheet of 8.5-by-11-inch construction paper and have them cut it in half. Take the half sheet and fold it in half (the long way/vertical). Punch a hole in the top and use some yarn to make a tassel.

Step 3. The template can be drawn on the chalkboard or it can be reproduced and displayed on an overhead projector. Not all of the characters are listed. This is just a template to get the students started. They can also add important quotes or symbols on one side and leave the characters on the other.

After Reading

Making Memories: A Scrapbooking Adventure for *Romeo and Juliet*

Objective: To promote visualization and extend students' understanding of *Romeo and Juliet.*

Materials: Three-ring folders, construction paper, colored paper, markers, colored pencils, tape, glue, stencils.

Step 1. This project could be completed during class time or it could be assigned for homework. The templates that are included in Chapter Four can be used for this project.

Step 2. Brainstorm with the students the key scenes or characters from the play.

Step 3. Instruct the students to select about five scenes or events. Character pages are also a valuable component for the scrapbook. (Refer to the "Key Scenes of Romeo and Juliet" handout).

Step 4. Once the pages are completed, the students are to bind their scrapbook pages and share them with their classmates.

Key Scenes in *Romeo and Juliet* for Scrapbook

Act 1, scene 1: The opening violence and fight between the families (provides much-needed background information)

Act 2, scene 2: The balcony scene (shows the emotions of the young lovers)

Act 3, scene 1: The death of Mercutio

Teaching the Classics in the Inclusive Classroom

Act 3, scene 5 (part 1): The morning when Romeo must leave, for he has been banished from Verona for murdering Mercutio

Act 3, scene 5 (part 2): The Capulets tell Juliet that she must marry Paris

Act 5, scene 3: Juliet's suicide

Romeo and Juliet Scrapbook Assessment Rubric

Category	4	3	2	1
Required elements	Scrapbook included all required elements as well as a few additional elements.	Scrapbook included all required elements and one additional element.	Scrapbook included all required elements.	One or more required elements were missing from the scrapbook.
Clarity and neatness	Scrapbook is easy to read and all elements are clearly written, labeled, or drawn.	Scrapbook is easy to read and most elements are clearly written, labeled, or drawn.	Scrapbook is hard to read with rough drawings and labels.	Scrapbook is hard to read and one cannot tell what goes where. The pages lack focus.
Use of time	Used time well during each class period with no teacher reminders.	Used time well during most class periods with no teacher reminders.	Used time well but required teacher reminders on one or more occasions to do so.	Used time poorly in spite of several teacher reminders to do so.
Content	All content is in the students' own words and is accurate.	Almost all content is in the students' own words and is accurate.	At least half of the content is in the students' own words and is accurate.	Less than half of the content is in the students' own words and/or is accurate.

Afterword: Teaching Literature for the Future

As we say at the beginning of this book, "Yes Virginia, *all students* can read the classics." Believe it or not, students might even enjoy them. Reading literature carries the potential to be a rewarding experience because language is power. When high school classrooms take advantage of the potentially empowering experience of the study of canonical literature, students become critical thinkers, writers, and readers. This is the mark of a truly engaging and effective literacy program, because students will become empowered if they experience for themselves the power of language and are encouraged to express their thoughts and experiences.

Both Langer (1995) and Rosenblatt (1995) describe classroom settings in which students are active and engaged participants in literature study. In these cases, students were allowed and encouraged to respond personally to their reading, with the support and encouragement of their teacher. The lessons and activities contained in the book promote a student-directed classroom. This is essential because when students know they are allowed and encouraged to use their voices in the classroom, this encourages them to explore texts more deeply.

A Few More Words About Democracy and Reader Response

We need to ask ourselves questions like these:

Do we value all children equally?

Is anyone more or less valuable?

What do we mean by *inclusion?*

Are there some children for whom inclusion is inappropriate?

As Rosenblatt has argued, her theoretical paradigm of reader response was her way of explaining the role and importance of democracy. Reader-response theory was developed at a time when communism and fascism were on the rise in Europe and the United States, and many other countries were fighting economic depression. There was real worry at the time that our notions of democracy and the individual voice were under threat. Rosenblatt believed, quite passionately, that to silence our students' voices was a tremendous disservice as they prepared to become adult participants in a democracy. If students were told how to think and feel, they would no longer develop their own ideas and personal positions. Instead, Rosenblatt wanted her students to develop their own ideas about the world. Literature was a catalyst and forum for the students' exploration. In a reader-response classroom (then and now), the students question, seek answers, and challenge their own ideas in a democratic forum where the teacher is the guide, not the ruler.

In light of this reminder about the merits of a democratic classroom and literacy learning, let us look again at the inclusion of students with special needs. These literature lessons and activities can meet the needs of both regular education students and students with special needs. These lessons are especially valuable, as they allow for curriculum differentiation and the individual education plans for students with special needs.

These lessons are the product of our own careful consideration of students with special needs; the instructional structure of these lessons and activities provides the flexibility for teachers to make changes based on individual skill development. The Council for Exceptional Children (CED) recommends that students with special needs who are included in a regular education classroom can meet the demands of the curriculum when appropriate adaptations are developed and implemented. In short, students with special needs can thrive in a regular education classroom when teachers recognize individual differences and create instruction in which all students can meet educational expectations. This includes the reading of classic literature. The lessons featured in this book employ multiple instructional strategies that can support a wide variety of student learning styles and differences in a regular education classroom that contains both regular education students and students with special needs.

Following are some suggested adaptations for students with special needs who are mainstreamed into the regular education classroom.

First, both the regular education and special education teacher need to complete a plan that addresses the specific educational needs and necessary adaptations for the mainstreamed students with special needs. They should communicate those adaptations to the parents. When the adaptation is no longer needed, it should be gradually removed.

As they do for regular education students, teachers should clearly articulate their goals and expectations to the students.

When creating lessons for teaching the literature classics, Howard Gardner's *Theory of Multiple Intelligences* should be incorporated. We highlighted these intelligences in relation to the lessons and activities that were developed for this volume; more than one type of intelligence is addressed in the lessons and activities described. Employing more than one intelligence is important for regular education students, but it is a *critical component* for students with special needs.

It is also important that

- Teachers provide a classroom environment that encourages reading and discussion for all students—regular education and mainstreamed students with special needs.
- Teachers ensure that instruction is detailed and presented in modalities other than orally.
- Students should have multiple opportunities to demonstrate what they have learned.
- Teachers must be consistent in expectations for all students and support them in reaching those expectations. Remember, we are creating a classroom that promotes successful teaching and learning for *all* students.

When we address the teaching of the classics in a middle or high school classroom, we need to approach it with the notions of democracy. How do we create a forum, like Rosenblatt's (and those who have followed in her footsteps), that encourages student participation and engagement? The activities and exercises in this book promote the participation of all students, not just the "regular kids." Students with special needs are a part of the democratic classroom. Instead of asking, "How can I teach those kids?" ask a better question: "How do I make my classroom more democratic, where *all* students have a voice?" The answer, we believe, is to promote student voice through engaging activities. That means no more study guides, no more multiple-choice quizzes. The world is far more interesting when there are many points of view and many possible answers, rather than just one.

Bibliography

Avenilla, F. R. (2003). Assessing the links between emotional and behavioral school engagement and academic outcomes among high school students. Unpublished doctoral dissertation, Pennsylvania State University.

Beach, R., & Marshall, J. (1990). *Teaching literature in the secondary school.* New York: Riverhead Books.

Beach, R., & Myers, J. (2001). *Inquiry-based English instruction: Engaging students in life and literature.* New York: Teachers College Press.

Beers, K. (2000). *Reading skills and strategies: Reaching reluctant readers.* Elements of Literature Series: Grades 6–12. Austin, TX: Holt, Rinehart & Winston.

Bloom, H. (1995). *The western canon.* New York: Riverhead.

Bolton, G. (1984). *Drama as education: An argument for placing drama at the centre of the curriculum.* London: Longman Group.

Bong, M. (2004). Academic motivation in self-efficacy, task value, achievement goal orientations, and attributional beliefs. *Journal of Educational Research, 97*(6), 287–298.

Braund, M. R. (1999). Using drama to improve student teachers' understanding in the physical sciences. (ED 436 402)

Britton, J. (1970). *Language and learning.* New York: Penguin.

Christenbury, L. (1994). *Making the journey: Being and becoming a teacher of English language arts.* Portsmouth, NH: Boynton/Cook.

Christenbury, L., & Kelly, P. P. (1983). *Questioning: A path to critical thinking.* Urbana, IL: ERIC Clearinghouse on Reading and Communication Skills, National Council of Teachers of English.

Elbow, P. (2002). *Writing with power* (2nd ed.). New York: Oxford University Press.

Fulwiler, T. (1987). *The journal book.* Upper Montclair, NJ: Boynton Cook.

Heathcote, D., & Bolton, G. (1994). *Drama for learning: Dorothy Heathcote's mantle of the expert approach to education.* Dimensions of drama series. Portsmouth, NH: Heinemann.

Heathcote, D., & Herbert, P. (1985). A drama of learning: Mantle of the expert. *Theory into Practice, 24*(3), 173–180.

Henry, M. (2000). Drama's ways of learning. *Research in Drama Education, 5*(1), 45–63.

Heston, S. (1999). *The Dorothy Heathcote archive.* Manchester, UK: Manchester Metropolitan University.

Innes, M., Moss, T., & Smigiel, H. (2001). What do the children say? The importance of student voice. *Research in Drama Education, 6*(2), 207–222.

Kamberelis, G., & Dimitriadis, G. (2005). *Qualitative inquiry: Approaches to language and literacy research.* New York: Teachers College Press.

Kariolides, N. (1992). The transactional theory of literature. In N. J. Kariolides (Ed.), *Reader response in the classroom: Evoking and interpreting meaning in literature* (pp. 21–32). White Plains, NY: Longman.

Kuzniewski, F., Sanders, M., Smith, G. S., Swanson, S., & Urich, C. (1998). *Using multiple intelligences to increase reading comprehension in English and math.* (ED 420 839)

Landy, R. J. (1982). *Handbook of educational drama and theatre.* Westport, CT: Greenwood Press.

Linnenbrink, E. A., & Pintrich, P. R. (2003). The role of self-efficacy beliefs in student engagement and learning in the classroom. *Reading and Writing Quarterly, 19*(2), 119–137.

McCammon, L. A., & Betts, D. (1999). *Helping kids to "imaginate": The story of drama education at one elementary school.* (ED 430 262)

Newmann, F. M. (1992). *Student engagement and achievement in American secondary schools.* New York: Teachers College Press.

Peck, D. (1989). *Novels of invitation: A guidebook for teaching literature to adolescents.* New York: Teachers College Press.

Pintrich, P. R., & De Groot, E. V. (1990). Motivational and self-regulated learning components of classroom academic performance. *Journal of Educational Psychology, 82*(1), 33–40.

Probst, R. (2004). *Response and analysis: Teaching literature in secondary school* (2nd ed.). Portsmouth, NH: Heinemann.

Ranger, L. (1995). *Improving reading comprehension through a multi-faceted approach utilizing drama.* (ED 380 758)

Roper, B., & Davis, D. (2000). Howard Gardner: Knowledge, learning, and development in drama and arts education. *Research in Drama Education, 5*(2), 217–233.

Rosenblatt, L. (1978). *The reader, the text, the poem: The transactional theory of the literary work.* Carbondale, IL: Southern Illinois University Press.

Rosenblatt, L. (1993). A performing art. In Daniel Sheridan (Ed.), *Teaching secondary English: Readings and applications* (pp. 52–59). White Plains, NY: Longman.

Rosenblatt, L. (1995). *Literature as exploration* (5th ed.). New York: Modern Language Association.

Ryan, R. M., & Deci, E. L. (2000). Self-determination theory and the facilitation of intrinsic motivation, social development, and well-being. *American Psychologist, 55*(1), 68–79.

Smith, F. (2004). *Understanding reading* (6th ed.). Mahwah, NJ: Erlbaum.

Vansteenkiste, M., Simons, J., Lens, W., Soenens, B., & Matos, L. (2005). Examining the motivational impact of intrinsic versus extrinsic goal framing and autonomy-supportive versus internally controlling communication style on early adolescents' academic achievement. *Child Development, 76*(2), 483–502.

Wilhelm, J. (1997). *You gotta be the book.* New York: Teachers College Press.

Wright, D. (2000). Drama education: A "self-organising system" in pursuit of learning. *Research in Drama Education, 5*(1), 23–32.

Yassa, N. A. (1999). High school involvement in creative drama. *Research in Drama Education, 4*(1), 37–50.

Index

References in italics refer to Tables and Figures

During-reading, 9–12
During-reading activities, 59–83; and character
    bookmarks, 75–79; and creating graphic novels,
    67–70; and found poetry, 80–83; and making text
    kinesthetic, 61–70; and reader's theater, 71;
    strategies and skill sets for, 60

E

Effective questions: characteristics of, 17
Efferent reading, 5
Elbow, P., 133
Elizabethan language, 2
Ellington Was Not a Street (Shange), 54
Emerson, R. W., 61
Englishonline.net, 166
Enron scandal, 39
Epic of Gilgamesh, 59, 109, 138; making text
    kinesthetic in, 61, 62; Project, 109; Rap, 109–110;
    sample script for, 63
Eyewitness Books, 54

F

Fall of the House of Usher'' (Poe)D
    81–82
Fascism, 191
Ferris Bueller's Day Off (film), 15
Fitzgerald, F. S., 1, 2, 4, 26
Found poetry, 80–83; lesson plan 1 for, 80–81;
    lesson plan 2 for, 81–82
Freevocabulary.com, 161
Freewriting, 134–135; lesson plan, 135 Tab. 5.8
Fulwiler, T., 118

G

Gardner, Howard, 192
Graphic novel, creating, 67–70; example, *69*; lesson
    plan, *70*; and *The Scarlet Letter,* 190; template, *68*
Graphic organizers, 161–166; and contextual word
    map template, *165*; vocabulary activities for, 161;
    and word chain template, *164*; and word detective
    template, *163*; and word map template, *162*
Great Britain, 148
Great Expectations (Dickens): and character
    bookmarks, 75
Great Gatsby, The (Fitzgerald), 1, 2, 4, 26
Green teacher, 2–3

H

Hamlet (Shakespeare), 4, 44, 75, 80
Hawthorne, N., 59, 67, 118–120
Hemingway, E., 1
Homer, 2, 31, 36, 59, 79
Hopkinson, D., 54
Hugo, V., 46

I

I Saw It activity, 107–108; lesson plan for, *107*; and
    The Scarlet Letter, 190
Inclusive public classroom, 3
Individual voice, 191–192
Invading words, 149–151; lesson plan, *149*; word se
    1, *150*; word set, 2, *150*; word set, 3, *151*
Iraq, U.S. military strike against, 49, 52
Iron Maiden, 32–33

J

Jane Eyre (Bronte), 157, 160
Journal writing, 118–125; academic benefits of, 119
    and creating and implementing journal prompts
    classroom, 120–121; and examples of weak journ
    prompts, 121; and follow-up discussion to journa
    entries, 122; and guidelines for creating effective
    journal prompts, 121; and journal prompts in
    action, 118–120

K

Kariolides, N., 11
Kelly, P. P., 18
Kinesthetic texts, making, 61–66; lesson plan for, 6
King Arthur and the Knights of the Round Table, 71–7
King, M. L., Jr., 49–52

L

Langer, S., 191
Lawson, Robert, 190
Lectures, teacher-directed, 16
Lee, H., 112
Lens, W., 10
Les Miserables (Hugo), 46
Letter from Birmingham Jail'' (King)D
    49, 50
Library of Congress, 102
Linnenbrink, E. A., 6
Literacy learning, 192
Literary canon, 3, 36
Literature letters, 136–137; lesson plan, *137*;
    template, *137*
Look Homeward, Angel (Wolfe), 1
Loser, 8

M

Macbeth (Shakespeare), 2, 4, 11, 44, 56, 85, 103, 11
    anticipation guide for, 56
Making memories, 100–101; lesson plan, 101; and
    Romeo and Juliet, 170, 188–189; and sample
    scrapbook page, 100
*Making the Journey: Being and Becoming a Teacher of
    English Arts* (Christenberry), 18
Mallory, Sir Thomas, 71
Mannis, C. A., 54